THE MINT

T. E. LAWRENCE is perhaps as human and yet as legendary a figure as emerged from World War I. During that war his activities were crucial in holding the Arabs on the side of the Allies. When he returned to England, he tried to lose his identity as a public figure and to forge a new life. In 1922 he enlisted in the RAF under the name of John Hume Ross and in 1927 he changed his name to T. E. Shaw. He finally left the RAF in March, 1935 and in May of that year he was killed in a motorcycling accident.

The Mint

NOTES MADE IN THE R.A.F. DEPOT

BETWEEN AUGUST AND DECEMBER, 1922,

AND AT CADET COLLEGE IN 1925 BY

T. E. Lawrence (352087 A/c ROSS)

REGROUPED AND COPIED IN 1927 AND

1928 AT AIRCRAFT DEPOT, KARACHI

The Norton Library

W · W · NORTON & COMPANY · INC ·

NEW YORK

First published in the Norton Library 1963 by
arrangement with Doubleday & Company, Inc.

Books That Live

The Norton imprint on a book means that in the publisher's
estimation it is a book not for a single season but for the years.
W. W. Norton & Company, Inc.

Printed in the United States of America

3 4 5 6 7 8 9 0

TO EDWARD GARNETT

You dreamed I came one night with this book
crying, 'Here's a masterpiece. Burn it.'

Well—*as you please*

CONTENTS

7

CONTENTS

CONTENTS

NOTE BY A. W. LAWRENCE

In 1922 T. E. Lawrence enlisted in the ranks of the R.A.F. under the name of John Hume Ross. From the Depot at Uxbridge he wrote to Edward Garnett on September the seventh of that year: 'I find myself longing for an empty room, or a solitary bed, or even a moment alone in the open air. However there is grand stuff here, and if I could write it . . .' In a later letter to Garnett he says that he has been making notes, 'scribbled at night, between last post and lights out, in bed.' They will make, he thinks, 'an iron, rectangular, abhorrent book, one which no man would willingly read.' In January 1923 he was discharged from the R.A.F. upon the discovery of his identity, but he was allowed to re-enter it two and a half years later, this time using the name of Shaw, under which he had meanwhile served in the Tank Corps. On re-enlistment he resumed the taking of notes.

In August 1927, writing from Karachi, he tells Garnett that he has cut up and arranged these notes in sections and is copying them seriatim into a notebook 'as a Christmas (which Christmas?) gift for you.' In manuscript, or in typescripts made from it, *The Mint* was read by a small number of people, including Bernard Shaw and E. M. Forster. On August 6, 1928, answering a letter from Forster, he wrote the longest account of the genesis of the book; it should be compared with that on p. 199. 'Every night in Uxbridge I used to sit in bed, with my knees drawn up under the blankets, and write on a pad the things of the day. I tried to put it all down, thinking that memory & time would sort them out, and enable me to select significant from insignificant. Time passed, five years and more (long enough, surely, for memory to settle down?) and at Karachi I took up the notes to make a book of them . . . and instead of selecting, I fitted into the book, somewhere & somehow, every single sentence I had written at Uxbridge.

'I wrote it tightly, because our clothes are so tight, and our lives so tight in the service. There is no freedom of conduct at all. Wasn't I right? G.B.S. calls it too dry, I believe. I put in little sentences of landscape (the Park, the Grass, the Moon) to relieve the shadow of servitude, sometimes. For service fellows there are no men on earth, except other service fellows . . . but we do see trees and star-light and animals, sometimes. I wanted to bring out the apartness of us.

'You wanted me to put down the way I left the R.A.F., and something about the Tanks. Only I still feel miserable at the time I missed because I was thrown out that first time. I had meant to go on to a Squadron, & write the real Air Force, and make it a book—a BOOK, I mean. It is the biggest subject I have ever seen, and I thought I could get it, as I felt it so keenly. But they broke all that in me, and I have been damaged ever since. I could never again recover the rhythm that I had learned at Uxbridge, resisting Stiffy . . . and so it would not be true to reality if I tried to vamp up some yarn of it all now. The notes go to the last day of Uxbridge, and there stop abruptly.

'The Cranwell part is, of course, not a part, but scraps. I had no notes for it . . . any more than I am ever likely to have notes of any more of my R.A.F. life. I'm it, now, and the note

12

season is over. The Cadet College part was vamped up, really, as you say, to take off the bitterness, if bitterness it is, of the Depot pages. The Air Force is not a man-crushing humiliating slavery, all its days. There is sun & decent treatment, and a very real measure of happiness, to those who do not look forward or back. I wanted to say this, not as propaganda, out of fairness, the phrase which pricked up your literary ears, but out of truthfulness. I set out to give a picture of the R.A.F., and my picture might be impressive and clever if I showed only the shadow of it . . . but I was not making a work of art, but a portrait. If it does surprisingly happen to be literature (I do not believe you there: you are partially kind) that will be because of its sincerity, and the Cadet College parts are as sincere as the rest, and an integral part of the R.A.F.

'Of course I know and deplore the scrappiness of the last chapters: that is the draw-back of memory, of a memory which knew it was queerly happy then, but shrank from digging too deep into the happiness, for fear of puncturing it. Our contentments are so brittle, in the ranks. If I had thought too hard about Cranwell, perhaps I'd have found misery there too. Yet I assure you that it seems all sunny, in the back view.

'Of Cadet College I had notes. Out on letters of Queen Alexandra's Funeral (Garnett praises that. Shaw says it's the meanness of a guttersnipe laughing at old age. I was so sorry and sad at the poor old queen), for the hours on guard, for the parade in the early morning. The Dance, the Hangar, Work and the rest were written at Karachi. They are reproductions of scenes which I saw, or things which I felt & did . . . but two years old, all of them. In other words, they are technically on a par with the manner of *The Seven Pillars:* whereas the Notes were photographs, taken day by day, and reproduced complete,

13

though not at all unchanged. There was not a line of the Uxbridge notes left out; but also not a line unchanged.

'I wrote *The Mint* at the rate of about four chapters a week, copying each chapter four or five times, to get it into final shape. Had I gone on copying, I should only have been restoring already crossed out variants. My mind seems to congest, after reworking the stuff several times.

'To insist that they are notes is not side-tracking. The Depot section was meant to be a quite short introduction to the longer section dealing with the R.A.F. in being, in flying work. Events killed the longer book: so you have the introduction, set out at greater length.'

In a subsequent letter to Forster he explained that he felt unable to publish the book because of 'the horror the fellows with me in the force would feel at my giving them away, at their "off" moments, with both hands. . . . So *The Mint* shall not be circulated before 1950.' But to Garnett he wrote: 'I took liberties with names and reduced the named characters of the squad from 50 odd to about 15.' (Since the extent of the 'liberties' is unknown, new names have been substituted in this edition in all passages which might have caused embarrassment or distress.)

The author portrays himself at a time when he was nervously exhausted, following the intense and almost continuous strain involved by the war, by the struggle for post-war settlement, by the writing of *Seven Pillars* and by writing the whole again after the theft of the original manuscript. Otherwise the starvation described in Chapter 1 would have been avoidable; as Colonel S. F. Newcombe points out, during some months before enlistment he received sufficient money to have enabled him to live comfortably, and in the last few weeks he caused some annoyance by constantly refusing invitations to meals and by fail-

14

ing to visit households at which he would have always been welcome. Presumably the years of over-exertion had resulted, when the need for activity ceased, in a condition of mind which allowed only negative decisions to be taken without intolerable effort. Life in the ranks, where a decision would never be required, therefore seemed the right solution, though to a man in such a state the rigours were bound to be magnified. The account of them, it need scarcely be said, was not written as propaganda for alleviating recruits' hardships; not till six years later was any part of the manuscript shown to an officer, after Garnett had received the completed book.

The typescript made at Garnett's order from the actual manuscript supplied the text for a few copies printed after the author's death (by Doubleday, Doran & Co., New York, 1936). Towards the end of his life, the author revised the book in a typescript re-copied from Garnett's, and therefore not absolutely identical. He made slight alterations on practically every page and an occasional substantial change. Evidence that he planned further corrections is extremely limited. He had noted two new possible titles for Part One, 'The Natural Man' and 'Enclosure,' to replace 'The Raw Material,' and for Part Two had scribbled 'Hammer and Anvil' as an alternative to the original title, 'In the Mill.' And in many passages he had substituted or discarded capital letters but failed to do so at every recurrence of the word. The present edition follows the revised text without the slips which he would have corrected, but for his accidental death. He intended, in fact, to print a limited edition himself on a hand-press, and had already obtained enough copies for its frontispiece of a reproduction (by Messrs. Emery Walker) of a portrait drawing by Augustus John, now in the Ashmolean Museum.

PART ONE

The Raw Material

1

RECRUITING OFFICE

God, this is awful. Hesitating for two hours up and down a filthy street, lips and hands and knees tremulously out of control, my heart pounding in fear of that little door through which I must go to join up. Try sitting a moment in the church-yard? That's caused it. The nearest lavatory, now. Oh yes, of course, under the church. What was Baker's story about the cornice?

A penny; which leaves me fifteen. Buck up, old seat-wiper: I can't tip you and I'm urgent. Won by a short head. My right shoe is burst along the welt and my trousers are growing fringes. One reason that taught me I wasn't a man of action was this routine melting of the bowels before a crisis. However, now we end it. I'm going straight up and in.

All smooth so far. They are gentle-spoken to us, almost sorry. Won't you walk into my parlour? Wait upstairs for medical exam? 'Righto!' This sodden pyramid of clothes upon the floor is sign of a dirtier man than me in front. My go next? Everything off? (Naked we come into the R.A.F.) Ross? 'Yes, that's me.'

Officers, two of them. . . .

'D'you smoke?'

19

Not much, Sir.

'Well, cut it out. See?'

Six months back, it was, my last cigarette. However, no use giving myself away.

'Nerves like a rabbit.' The Scotch-voiced doctor's hard fingers go hammer, hammer, hammer over the loud box of my ribs. I must be pretty hollow.

'Turn over: get up: stand under here: make yourself as tall as you can: he'll just do five foot six, Mac: chest—say 34. Expansion—by Jove, 38. That'll do. Now jump: higher: lift your right leg: hold it there: cough: all right: on your toes: arms straight in front of you: open your fingers wide: hold them so: turn round: bend over. Hullo, what the hell's those marks? Punishment?' 'No Sir, more like persuasion Sir, I think.' Face, neck, chest, getting hot.

'H . . . m . . . m . . . , that would account for the nerves.' His voice sounds softer. 'Don't put them down, Mac. Say *Two parallel scars on ribs*. What were they, boy?'

Superficial wounds, Sir.

'Answer my question.'

A barbed-wire tear, over a fence.

'H . . . m . . . m . . . and how long have you been short of food?'

(O Lord, I never thought he'd spot that. Since April I've been taking off my friends what meals I dared, all that my shame would let me take. I'd haunt the Duke of York steps at lunch-time, so as to turn back with someone to his club for the food whose necessity nearly choked me. Put a good face on it; better.)

Gone a bit short the last three months, Sir. How my throat burns!

'More like six' . . . came back in a growl. The worst of

telling lies naked is that the red shows all the way down. A long pause, me shivering in disgrace. He stares so gravely, and my eyes are watering. (Oh, it hurts: I wish I hadn't taken this job on.)

At last, 'All right: get back into your clothes. You aren't as good as we want but after a few weeks at the Depot you'll pull up all right.' Thank you very much, Sir. 'Best of luck, boy,' from Mac. Grunt from the kinder-spoken one. Here's the vegetable market again, not changed. I'm still shaking everyway, but anyhow I've done it. Isn't there a Fuller's down that street? I've half a mind to blow my shilling on a coffee. Seven years now before I need think of winning a meal.

2

THE GATE

Our sergeant, trimly erect in creaseless blue uniform, hesitated as we left the station yard. Your fighting-man is shy of giving orders to people possibly disobedient, for an ignored command disgraces would-be authority; and Englishmen (being what they are) resent being bossed except as law or imperious circumstance directs. Then in unconvincing offhand, 'I'm going over to that shop a moment. You fellows keep along this foot-path till I give you a shout,' and he crossed the sunny street to pop slickly in and out of a tobacconist's. I suppose he has done such conducting duty daily for months: but he needn't care for the feelings of us six shambling ones. We are moving in a dream.

This main street of an old-fashioned country town clanks with hulking trams labelled Shepherd's Bush. Invaders. We walk till on our left rise the bill-boards of eligible plots and heavy elms bulge through the wall of a broken park. The tyre-polished tarmac glistens before and after these umbrellas of shade. Here is a gateway, high and brick-pillared with bombs atop: and by it a blue sentry with a rifle. A momentary drawing-together of our group. But head in air on the opposite pavement the sergeant strides forward, looking hard to his front. The stone flags ring under the ferrule of his planted stick.

Our sun-softened asphalt declines into a dusty gravel. Shuffle shuffle goes the loose crowd of us, past another gate. The wall gives place to park-paling and wire: there are khaki men in the park, distant. A third gate. The sergeant crosses towards it, heading us off. With a wave of his stick he shepherds our little mob past the sentry who stands firm before a box. For a moment we glance back over the bayonet at the gleaming road with its traffic and its people strolling, freely, in a world that we have quitted.

3

IN THE PARK

They licensed us to wander where we pleased (within gates) through the still autumn afternoon. The clouded breadth of the fallen park, into which this war-time camp had been intruded, made an appeal to me. Across it lay the gentle curve of Park Road, the only formal road in camp and quiet, being out of bounds. With a blue smoothness it stretched between cut lawns, under a rank of trees.

The park dipped in the middle to the ragged edges of a little stream, and huts climbed down each slope from the tops, reaching out over the valley as if they had meant to join roofs across its leafy stream—but something, perhaps the dank, deep grass of the lowland meadows, stayed them.

I paused on the bridge above the stagnant water, which wound into the hollow between banks of thicketed rush and foxglove. By each side were choice-planted great trees. On the western slope swelled the strident activity of red-and-chocolate footballers. Should I be concerned in football again? There had been a rumour of that sinful misery, forced games. The ball at intervals plonked musically against men's boots or on the resistant ground: and each game was edged by its vocal border of khaki and blue. The blue clothes, which pinked their wearers' faces, seemed of a startling richness against the valley-slopes of verdant or yellow grass. Curtains of darkness were drawn around the playing fields by other bulky trees, from whose boughs green shadows dripped.

The particular wilderness of the Pinne's banks seemed also forbidden to troops: in its sallows sang a choir of birds. From the tall spire (where it pricked black against the sky on the ridge behind the pent-roofed camp) fell, quarter by quarter, the Westminster chimes on tubular bells. The gentleness of the river's air added these notes, not as an echo, but as an extra gravity and sweetness, to its natural sounds and prolonged them into the distances, which were less distant than silvered with the deepening afternoon and the mists it conjured off the water. The dragging rattle of electric trains and trams, outside the pale, emphasised the aloof purposefulness in which so many men were cloistered here.

By tea-time the football grew languid, and at last ceased. Slowly the mist invaded the lowest ground and slowly it climbed all the grass slope until the lights of the camp were glowing direct into its sea.

4

THE FEAR

After dusk the camp paths became thronged with men, all seeming friends, who met with a freemasonry of unintelligible greeting. I shrank from them and equally from their canteen with its glare and its hospitable smells. The thought of our hut returned to me as a refuge. Thankfully I made for it.

When I opened the door the long interior with its pendent lights offered indeed a refuge against the night. Its colouring was gay:—primary white walls sectioned by pilasters of hot brick, or by slender roof-posts painted green aligning themselves over the concrete floor between the close rows of brown-blanketed identical beds. But there was no one there, and the roof seemed full of staring eyes. I stumbled dizzily, under their view, down the alley of polished linoleum which lay like a black gangway across the concrete. Did the floor pitch slightly, with a rise and fall, like a deck? Or was my head swimming in the brilliant silence which thronged the empty place?

I lay, sickly, on my allotted bed. For a moment my bedfellow was perfect fear. The globes stared unwinking; my external imaginings flocked to the pillow and whispered to each ear that I was attempting the hardest effort of my life. Could a man, who for years had been closely shut up, sifting his inmost self with painful iteration to compress its smallest particles into a book—could he suddenly end his civil war and live the open life, patent for everyone to read?

Accident, achievement, and rumour (cemented equally by my partial friends) had built me such a caddis-shell as almost prompted me to forget the true shape of the worm inside. So I had sloughed them and it right off—every comfort and possession—to plunge crudely amongst crude men and find myself for these remaining years of prime life. Fear now told me that nothing of my present would survive this voyage into the unknown.

Voyage? Yes, the long hold-like hall had the sheer and paint-smell and sense of between decks. The pillars and tie-beams of its louring roof barred it into stalls like the stalls of a cattle boat waiting its load. Awaiting us.

Slowly we drifted in, those who had come with me today, till on the made-up beds five or six of us were lying subdued to the strangeness and the silence: a silence again pointed by that faint external creeping roar of the tramcars which swung along the road behind. Subtly our presences comforted one another.

At ten o'clock the door was flung open and a torrent of others entered, those stagers who had been here for some days and had gained outward assurance. They fought off nervousness by noise, by talk, by Swanee River on the mouth-organ, by loose scrummaging and japes and horseplay. Between the jangles of sudden song fell bars of quiet, in which man whispered confidentially to man. Then again the chatter, a jay-laugh, that pretence of vast pleasure from a poor jest. As they swiftly stripped for sleep a reek of body fought with beer and tobacco for the mastery of the room. The horseplay turned to a rough-house: snatching of trousers, and smacks with the 27 flat of hard hands, followed by clumsy steeplechases over the obstacles of beds which tipped or tilted. We, the last joined, were trembling to think how we should bear the freedom of this fellowship, if they played with us. Our hut-refuge was become libertine, brutal, loud-voiced, unwashed.

At ten-fifteen lights out; and upon their dying flash every sound ceased. Silence and the fear came back to me. Through the white windows streaked white diagonals from the conflicting arc-lamps without. Within there ruled the stupor of first sleep, as of embryons in the natal caul. My observing spirit slowly and deliberately hoisted itself from place to prowl across this striped upper air, leisurely examining the forms stretched out so mummy-still in the strait beds. Our first lesson in the Depot had been of our apartness from life. This second vision was of our sameness, body by body. How many souls gibbered that night in the roof-beams, seeing it? Once more mine panicked, suddenly, and fled back to its coffin-body. Any cover was better than the bareness.

Night dragged. The sleepers, their prime exhaustion sated, began to stir uneasily. Some muttered thickly in the false life of dreams. They moaned or rolled slowly over in their beds, to the metallic twangling of their mattresses of hooked wire. In sleep on a hard bed the body does not rest without sighing. Perhaps all physical existence is a weary pain to man: only by day his alert stubborn spirit will not acknowledge it.

The surge of the trams in the night outside lifted sometimes to a scream as the flying wheels gridded on a curve. Each other hour was marked by the cobbling tic-tac of the relief guard, when they started on their round in file past our walls. Their rhythmic feet momently covered the rustling of the great chestnuts' yellowed leaves, the drone of the midnight rain, and the protestant drip drip of roof-drainings in a gutter.

28

For two or three such periods of the night I endured, stiff-stretched on the bed, widely awake and open-eyed, realising myself again one of many after the years of loneliness. And the morrow loomed big with our new (yet certainly not smooth) fate in store. 'They can't kill us, anyhow,' Clarke had said at tea-time. That might, in a way, be the worst of it. Many men would take the death-sentence without a whimper to escape the life-sentence which fate carries in her other hand. When a plane shoots downward out of control, its crew cramp themselves fearfully into their seats for minutes like years, expecting the crash: but the smoothness of that long dive continues to their graves. Only for survivors is there an after-pain.

5

FIRST DAY

The morning passed with us lolling here and there on imperfect pursuits. Breakfast and dinner were sickening, but ample. Without being told we set to and cleaned the hut. The voluntariness of our mob astonished me: I had expected sullenness, in reaction against the nervous effort of enlistment. Certainly we all still funked our prospect and hung about distractedly heartening one another, a dozen times over, with the same vain summary. ' 'Tasn't bin so baad. 'Tisn't goin' to be too bad, d'y'think?' Though we can see in the eyes of the drilling recruits that is surely is. Groups of us pressed round any man with a rumour or experience to repeat.

Testing and examination went on, intermittently. The R.A.F. standards were severe—more so than the Army's—and many of us found difficulties. The supervising officer was prompting his rejects to go up elsewhere for some regiment. Those he had passed came back to the hut confessing their success with good-humoured rueful resignation: but in secret, they were proud. Those who failed saw yellow and thanked their stars—too loudly to convince us. On the credit side was our laughing, our candour, our creeping obedience: on the other side the uncanny gentleness of sergeants and officers whenever we met them. Always I thought of the spider and its flies. Around us, for the rest, the unheeding camp lived its life to a trumpet code and a rhythm of bells like ships' bells.

In the afternoon I was called, set to a table, and told to write an essay on the birth-place which I'd not seen since six weeks old! I did what any infant in my place would do—improvised gaily. 'You'll do,' said the Lieutenant, liking my prose.[1] He handed me to a bald-headed officer whose small eyes must have been paining him: for he had taken off his glasses and repeatedly pursed his eyes in a tight grimace, while he put me through a stiff catechism. London had told me my formalities were over, bar the swearing-in, so I was taken by surprise and in unreadiness shifted my feet and stammered parts of a history. He got very impatient and banged out, 'Why were you doing nothing during the war?'

'Because I was interned, Sir, as an alien enemy.' 'Great Scott, and you have the nerve to come to ME as a recruit—what prison were you in?' 'Smyrna, in Turkey, Sir.' 'Oh. What . . . why? As a British subject! Why the hell didn't you say so directly? Where are your references, birth certificate, educational papers?' 'They kept them in Maria Street, Sir. I understood they signed me on there.' *'Understood!* Look here, m'lad. You're trying to join the Air Force, so get it into your head right away that you're not wanted to understand anything before you're told. Got it?' Then his eye fell on my papers in his file, where the acceptance I had stated was plainly set forth. He waved me wearily away. 'Get outside there with the others, and don't waste my time.'

[1] Three years later and wearing a different shape I came before the supervising officer, to be set an essay on Sport. As he read my disfavouring of all sports he called me out and questioned, 'Were you here some years ago under a different name? And did you then write me an essay about the sea-side of Wales?'

As we waited in the passage for the oath which would bind us (we waited two hours, a fit introduction to service life which is the waiting of forty or fifty men together upón the leisure of any officer or N.C.O.), there enwrapped us, never to be lost, the sudden comradeship of the ranks;—a sympathy born half of our common defencelessness against authority (authority which could be, as I had just re-learnt, arbitrary) and half of our true equality: for except under compulsion there is no equality in the world.

The oath missed fire: it babbled of the King; and, with respect, no man in the ranks today is royalist after the antique sense in which the Georgian army felt itself peculiarly the King's. We do certainly observe some unformulated loyalty with heart and soul: but our ideal cannot have legs and a hat. We have obscurely grown it, while walking the streets or lanes of our country, and taking them for our own.

After all was over a peace came upon us. We had forced ourselves so far against the grain, our unconscious selves rebelliously hoping for some accident to reject us. It was like dying a death. Reason calls the grave a gateway of peace: and instinct shuns it.

When we had sworn and signed our years away, the sergeant marched us back to the hut. There seemed a new ring about his voice. We collected our tiny possessions and moved to another hut, apart from the unsigned men. A sober-faced corporal counted us in. His welcome was the news that henceforward, for weeks, there would be no passes for us nor liberty to go through the iron gates. The world went suddenly distant. Our puzzled eyes peered through the fence at its strangeness, wondering what had happened. In the evening we began to talk about 'civilians.'

6

US

Our hut is a fair microcosm of unemployed England: not of unemployable England, for the strict R.A.F. standards refuse the last levels of the social structure. Yet a man's enlisting is his acknowledgment of defeat by life. Amongst a hundred serving men you will not find one whole and happy. Each has a lesion, a hurt open or concealed, in his late history. Some of us here had no money and no trade, and were too proud to join the ranks of labour's unskilled. Some faltered at their jobs, and lost them. The heart-break of seeking work (for which each day's vain tramp unfitted them yet further) had driven many into the feeble satisfaction of 'getting in.' Some have blacked their characters and hereby dodge shame or the police court. Others have been tangled with women or rejected by women and are revenging the ill-usage of society upon their smarting selves. Yet aloud we all claim achievement, moneyed relatives, a colourful past.

We include 'lads' and their shady equivalent, the hard case. Also the soft and silly: the vain: the old soldier, who is lost without the nails of service: the fallen officer, sharply contemptuous of our raw company, yet trying to be well-fellow and not proud. Such a novice dips too willingly at the dirty jobs, while the experienced wage-slave stands by, grumbling.

The dressy artisans, alternately allured and repelled by our unlimited profession, dawdle for days over their trade tests, hoping some accident will make up their minds. Our Glasgow blacksmith, given only bread for tea one day in dining hall, cried, 'Aam gaen whame,' muddled his trial-job and was instantly turned down. That last afternoon he spent spluttering crazy non-intelligible confidences at every one of us. A dumpy lad he was, with tear-stained fat cheeks, and so glad to have failed. 'Dry bread,' he would quiver half-hourly with a sob in his throat. Simple-minded, like a child; but stiff-minded, too, and dirty; very Scotch.

The 'axed' Devonport apprentices, just out of their papers, despise our mob. They have worked in a shop with men. Two barmen sleep beside Boyne, ex-captain in the K.R.R. Opposite lies the naval suburb:—a Marconi operator, R.N., and two able seamen, by their own tale. Ordinary seamen, perhaps. Sailors talk foul and are good everyday sorts. The G.W.R. machinist rejected all kindness, and swilled beer solitarily. There were chauffeurs (read 'vanmen') enlisted for lorry work: some dapper-handed clerks, sighing at the purgatory of drill between them and their quiet stools-to-be: a small tradesman out of Hoxton, cherishing his overdrawn bank book as proof of those better days: photographers, mechanics, broken men; bright lads from school, via errand-running. Most are very fit, many keen on their fresh start here, away from reputation. All are alert when they have a shilling in pocket, and nothing for the while to do.

Men move in or out of our hut daily, so that it flickers with changing faces. We gain a sense of nomadity. No one dare say, 'Here I will sleep tonight, and this I will do on the morrow,' for we exist at call.

Our leading spirits are China and Sailor, Sailor taking the

curt title because he is more of a sailor than all the naval pre-
tenders put together. A lithe, vibrant ex-signaller of the war-
time, quicksilvery even when he (seldom) stands still. Not tall
but nervous on his feet, a Tynesider who has seen many ships
and ports and should be qualified as a hard case. Yet good-
humour bubbles out of him and in drink he is embodied kindness. With his fists he is a master. His voice renders his fre-
quent bursts of song our delight, for even in speech it is of a
purring richness with a chuckle of reckless mirth latent in the
throat behind his soberest word. Sailor's vitality made him
leader of our hut after the first hour.

China, his sudden pal, is a stocky Camberwell coster-
monger, with the accent of a stage Cockney. Since childhood
he has fought for himself and taken many knocks, but no care
about them. He is sure that safety means to be rough among
the town's roughs. His deathly-white face is smooth as if waxed,
the bulging pale eyes seem lidless like a snake's, and out of
their fixedness he stares balefully. He is knowing. When Sailor
starts a rag, China produces a superb haw-haw voice that takes
off the officer-type into pure joy, with a subtle depth of mim-
icry. He is always President in our mock courts-martial.

Normally his speech is a prolonged snarl, as filely-grating
as his pal's is melodious. China has said 'fuck' so often, inlay-
ing it monotonously after every second word of his speech with
so immense an aspirated 'f,' that his lips have pouted to it in
a curve which sneers across his face like the sound-hole of a
fiddle's belly. Sailor and China, the irrepressibles, fascinate me
with the attraction of unlikeness: for I think I fear animal
spirits more than anything in the world. My melancholy ap-
proaches me nearer to our sombre conscientious hut-corporal,
whom everybody hates for his little swearing and inelasticity.
But he is old, and years, with their repetition, sap the fun
from any care-full man.

7

THE NEW SKIN

      Rumour has it that today we draw our kit. From breakfast-time we hang about in excitement; hoping to lose, with these our old suits, the instant reminder that we have been civvies: and to escape the disdain we now read in the eyes of uniformed men.

Rumour at last turns true. In fours we march to the Q.M. Stores and there stand up against a hail of clothing flung at us by six sweating storemen, while the quartermaster, upright behind his counter, intoned the list. But the list stood on its head . . . socks, pairs, three; it ran like that . . . so nobody could know what was what.

We shouldered the kit-bag, draped the tunics and trousers (khaki, alas!) over one arm, hugged the blue clothes, our ambition, with the other; and were chivied to the boot-store where we tried on as many as we could grab of the hundreds of boots upon the floor. At last each had two pairs, fairly fitting, but barge-heavy, and stiff as cast-iron. The boot-man hung them round our necks by their strings, and we staggered to the tailors who next took hold of us that they might chalk alterations on the seams of our blue tunics. Laden with all else of the mighty kit we steered our way back up the camp roads to the hut.

'Quick!' cried Corporal Abner. 'Into your khaki: yes, it'll fit. Of course: all khaki fits—where it touches. You're to get shot of your civvy duds before dinner.' Straightway the staff of the reception hut were transformed into old-clothes' merchants. Our hut swarmed with senior airmen, fingering or looking, appraising, disparaging, bidding. Some optimists posted their suits home for use on leave but to most of us home looks long years away, and leave improbable. 'Puttees on,' insisted the Corporal: 'puttees always in working hours.' We wanted to weep while we pulled the harsh trousers as high as our knees and wound the drab puttee from boot-top upward, till it gripped the trouser-hem above the calf. Then we pulled the slack of the trouser dropsically down again over the puttee to hide the join. It did more than hide the join: it hid the reality of our legs and was hot, tight and hideous, like an infantryman's rig. When we had finished dressing we were silenced by our new slovenliness. The hut of normal men had gone, and barbarous drab troops now filled it.

'Fall in' from the Corporal then, slowly, almost reluctantly. What new thing was coming our way? Off we raggedly clopped past the butcher's and the tailor's, to halt before the barber's door. 'First two men,' and in they went. The hasty barber, one eye on the clock of his lunch, ran his clippers up and over our heads. Three slashes with the scissors jagged our top hair to match the plucked staircase of the back. 'Next two,' yelled the barber's fatigue man. Forty before dinner-bugle. Would he do it? Easy. Back in the sheltering hut we gazed again without comment at the botch of bristles upon each other's pale scalps: and were reconciled to imprisonment in the Depot for a while. It's not tempting to be a figure of fun in the streets.

Khaki is prison garb here, the gate-sentry not letting out a man who wears it. So we are confined till the tailors release 37 our altered blue. In our brief lives few of us have been locked up before, and the very feel of it makes an uncreased wing begin to beat against the bars. One adventurer slipped down to the tailors, after dark, and brought word that half a dollar will secure priority, and even a bob do something: otherwise the tailors are so busy that it may be a fortnight before they can deliver. A fortnight! We have been here three days and it feels like ever.

The afternoon passes in a first effort to stow our kit after the Corporal's manner, to black the stubbornly-brown boots and to smear brown clay (blanco) over the web equipment with which, in marching order, the airman is harnessed against any wanderlust that might make him yearn to go forth without his all upon his back, like a snail. We make a mess of each single task: and wonder despairingly what will happen as our squad goes on square in such amateur fashion. 'Square,' snorted Corporal Abner in derision, as though the square was a privilege of angels—'You are for fatigues tonight.'

8

OFFICERS' MESS

Tonight at six sees us falling in, thrilled, for our first uniformed parade, raw boots, flat hats and all. The older the airman, the sloppier may he wear the rim of his cap. Our prentice legs in the rasping trousers and bulky puttees swung against each other like baby elephants. The dingy overalls which further deformed our shapes were cross-creased from the bale. Gone with our civvies was the civility of the sergeants. Flight Lawton's vindicating stick fell, not too lightly, on my shoulder. 'You, you, you,' he ticked us off. 'Officers' mess. Jump to it.' We wheeled away, bear-driven by the duty corporal to a softly-shining door.

Our leader entered, looked back, beckoned us inside. Before the kitchen-range stood a shirt-sleeved batman, Irish, red-headed and huge, dressing in breeches to go out. One leg was propped on a chair, while he rubbed a wet rag at a stain on its threadbare ample thigh. 'Two in there,' he spluttered, pointing to the main kitchen. 'Ye two wash up': but the spick-and-span genius of the scullery waved us away. 'Fatigue men? I've shit 'em,' he said.

'Saucy cunt,' grumbled Red-Head, scratching it: then he opened the door into a yard which gave light to the three great windows of a passage. Their panes were spotted with the   39 scales of old frosting. 'Get these clean.' From a closet came leathers, dusters, a backless chair to stand on. The paint-spots were like isinglass, and had to be scraped off singly with a knife. Red-Head often passed, cheering our futility with horse-noises from his mouth.

In the passage behind my back stood a boxed telephone. Each time the bell rang its batman stepped to it. His callers were generally cronies. We heard snatches of Blackpool, of the Spurs' prospects, of Sunderland, or of winning horses in the older but little esteemed sport. Through the swing-doors came an officer's head, more often officers' voices. Sherry and bitters, gin and bitters, martinis, vergins, vermouths. 'Three whisky sodas *quickly*'—whose familiar harsh voice was that? My trade-test officer. The bartender splashed full his glasses and hurried to and fro. As he passed the telephone box he would reach a long arm, beer-laden, quickly into its depth.

We had finished the windows: but our fatigue must last till nine. 'Come in here,' called Red-Head, through a full mouth, and we returned to the pantry. Its deal-topped table (on good legs of oak) was spread with grease-spotted sheets of the *Star*. The rout of the Greek Army jostled the dead Duchess of Albany in the headlines. The cook produced a much used plate of butter, an end of jam, and bread:—relics of the mess tea. 'Scran up.' We set to and wolfed. Two other batmen entered, with heaped plates of cold bacon and potato salad. Red-Head sluiced his share with vinegar. Noisily they shovelled the stuff away with the broad of their knives—a fine art. We watched it go. Three glasses of beer were brought, with an old pack of cards. They cut and the penalty was drinks. The telephone's servant joined the rest. Again they cut. 'Lost, fuck it,' he grumbled and went out, to return beaming. 'Fucking bar's shut.' Laughter. Red-Head belched loudly, trying with one hand to still his kicking belly.

He was too full of food, and disgustedly banged his ravaged plate along the table at us, with a grunt. 'Muck in.' We did, yet still looked lean. 'You bloody swaddies can't half yaffle,' said he, enviously. 'Chuck 's that bread.' He hacked it thick, loaded the slabs with fat bacon, and rubbed them on the table where the vinegar had spilled. While we worked at this new luck they still talked of football, drinks and officers. 'Who's here tonight?' asked our taskmaster of the operator. 'Old man,' was the sufficient and meaning reply. The veriest recruit knew that 'old man' was the Commandant, the stark skull and crossbones under which the Depot sailed. 'The bastard!' swore Red-Head: he lifted the stock-pot's lid, and spat in neatly. 'A gob for his guts: soup's as rich as old nick.' He took his cap and went.

An hour later we slipped back to our hut and were heroes of the night, for we had the longest yarn and alone had made a meal out of our job. First post came: last post. The plangent beauty of these night-calls putting duties behind us for eight hours and giving us the delight of a half-hour's bed before sleep:—a half-hour in which the relaxed body, free of its scratchy clothes and clumping boots, stretches itself between the smooth sheets, without censure. Then lights out—the nightly miracle which brought darkness, and silence with the pale moon to rule our boiling hut.

9

P.T.

Corporal Abner looked up suddenly, with that queer twist of the mouth which might be derision or might be pity, and said, 'You're for P.T. tomorrow: a quarter-past six.' The shades are closing inch by inch. *It's this exercise I fear. My body is not worth much, now.* The others put on a braver face. 'I'm glad we're going to get drill,' said Park: 'it'll take the slouch out of us.' 'Yes,' chimed in Madden, always quick to follow a lead, 'sort of thing the civvies in London pay fifty quid for, we get harry-freeman's.'

In a hollow dawn (there is early cocoa at the cook-house, but fellows on P.T. can't, in the quarter of an hour's dressing time, run so far and queue up for it) we fall in outside the hut. Our trousers are belted round us with knotted braces and their leg bottoms tucked into our socks. Rolled-up sleeves, of course, and rubber shoes. We are marched to the asphalt square whose smoothness is made skiddy, on such moist days, by its scattered grit. Across it the five hundred of us are spread in open order. Physical training is based on the assumption that the men are asleep or careless, or shirkers. It is an affair of suddennesses: starts and turns, cries, pitfalls and checks. Our fifty are as keen as wild mustard, but timorous for the first day. Many made mistakes and were bawled at till they grew rattled and became the easier victims. To a cool head, the instructors' over-careful precautions gave them away. We quickly learned to meet or avoid their onset. 'Bluff or scrounge,' was the old hands' proverb as they put us wise to labour-saving wrinkles, taking for granted that we were out to make the laziest of a tolerable job. Today; as it happens, we aren't: but tomorrow we shall be. Infection grows.

'Dismiss,' and we were panting on our beds for the ten minutes before breakfast. The fumes of sweat expanded broadly from our wet waistbands and clinging shirts. I missed breakfast because my breathing hurt me. After that Handley crash in Rome the X-ray showed one rib, furred like the bristles of a toothbrush, against the wall of my chest: and much lung-pumping taps its thin dagger-pain into my heart. When the trembling stopped I swallowed some water from the wash-house tap, and was better. We kicked our way into overalls, and paraded for fatigues.

The stick came down and cut off me and Park. 'Butcher's shop,' said Flight Sergeant Walker. *Sounds as if my luck was out this morning.* Distaste for the sight and feel and smell of raw flesh has made me almost a vegetarian. The butcher is a young corporal, face white and full as a bladder of lard, and his bloodied overalls smell of the trade. Thank heaven he does not want us in the shop. We are to fill and stoke the two boilers outside the door. In half an hour they are full of water, which is getting warm. He shows us by the ditch behind the shop, under a clipped thorn-hedge, heaps of the cut-open sacks in which his frozen carcasses had travelled. These we are to wash.

They must have been long lying there, for they were pressed solid, and stuck together. When we dragged at them they tore. Their insides were earwigged, maggoty and worm-full. Park 43 found a hedge-stake and prised the stinking layers apart over the grass: happy-looking grass, for it was rankly, greenly uncut and irregular, in the waste triangle behind the butchery.

We were to have treated each sack separately; but the damp ground had so conspired with the salt of the meat and the hedge-drippings against the cloth that it rotted away in our hands. Therefore with our stakes we forked lumps at a time into the coppers. The water boiled and we poled the sackings around under it till they were pliant. Then, fishing them out by sections, we impaled them on the quickset spikes where they steamed with an ardent soupy smell into the mist which was today's weather. The corporal came out rubbing his hands and sniffing our hedge which two hours' work had made mouldy with old jute. 'Good work,' said he, 'you can throw away the lot now.' 'Well I'm fucked,' gasped my half-section, at this futile issue of our toil.

'Posh job, Park,' said I, to tease him. Park, an embryo transport driver, with the swank of a failure calls himself an ex-Brooklands racing mechanic—to gild his degraded present by reflection. He has been at the least a garage-boy; and feels himself a tradesman and unionist. The tradesman has tremendous contempt for the class which knows no trade. So Park could not take refuge in my irony against misemployment as a labourer. Instead he stood up tally, and cursed the Depot and the job and the butcher-corporal and himself and the Army and Navy and Royal Air Force, while the smoke of our coppers vomited into the heavy air and rained down in a black whirl around our faces. 'Steady, Park, you'll curse the fire out.' 'Fuck the fire!' he cried, crashing a heavy boot against the stove door. The butchers came out to see what was the matter. 'Better change the water: that lot's a bit fruity,' ordered the corporal innocently.

Sack-boiling had been his brain-wave to keep at work the fatigue men whom his policy requisitioned daily from headquarters, as proof of the busy-ness of his shop. Headquarters willingly obliged him, for such grinds chastened the hot hearts of their many recruits till they longed even for 'square,' for that extremest severity of drill and discipline which alone could qualify them to leave the Depot. Because it is a Depot the recruits must be chased. 'Here we tame lions,' boast the instructors at us. But we are very lambs and the regimen of lions strikes hard on lambs.

The corporal did no more than he was told in keeping us foolishly engaged all the wet day. We fetched gallons of water and boiled it over more coke: and flung in worse and worse chunks of sacking till our stew was as much worms as cloth. Still he was insatiable and nagged at us till we banged the stoves to drown his voice and stoked sparks out of the chimney pipes. Euclid, that labourer of the obvious, was driven into tender heads to toughen them. This fatigue was a physical Euclid to each us our worthlessness. We had enlisted in hope that our improving hands might aid those who strove against the air. A month, two months of this, and we will accept the Force's verdict that our time weighs the same whether we work or waste it. Then will we present to our instructors a blank grey sheet, on which to draw up, by drill and instant obedience, an airman. Let us see if the Air Force can build as well as it has destroyed.

10

LAST POST

With the startling blast of first post at 9.30 p.m. the hut door is banged violently back. A stick clatters across its panels, with the roar of 'Orderly Corporal.' We spring to the foot of our beds and line up there, end to end of the hut, bareheaded, stiffly at attention, silent. The corporal strides round, noting for report the name over any ownerless bed. Then we tear off boots and slacks and socks, and prop ourselves in bed luxuriously on an elbow, to continue the talk which has been for many evenings marching with the next fellow, a yard away. The babel is many-themed and not all conversational. On two beds at the end are two late visitors to the coffee-stall cramming sandwiches tightly into their mouths. Next them Peters is brushing his boots. He has been, for the last half-hour: these our boots are new with grease and the order is that they shall shine at once, if not sooner. So we polish hour after hour and scrape and bone them desperately with the handles of our toothbrushes and run about after every old-soldier's nostrum of blacking or potato juice or fire or polish or hot water.

In some near beds is grouped a concert party singing, now 'Rock of Ages' and now:

> *You took the sunshine from our alley*
> *When you said GOOD-BYE.*

Every man in the hut, bar me, tries shamelessly or shamefully to sing and hum and whistle: and every sort of song goes up at once till two or three voices chance upon one favourite or till that with the most marked rhythm prevails. Then for a minute we have a roaring chorus supported with mess-tin lids and banged boxes. Always there is melody in the hut. Something to which you can tap the foot.

Beyond the concert our sombre corporal is making up a return, bending close over his sheet in the imperfect light. Elsewhere more are eating: two, tired, are already face-down on the pillows: while Dickson in bed, fully dressed and flat on his back, is reciting the 'Ancient Mariner' slowly and particularly. He has been to the wet canteen: and much beer always calls the Mariner out of him. Through the hubbub Sailor and China our champion obscenists are bandying curses across the hut's central bar which hides the twenty-six beds on that side from the twenty-six on this. Someone on the far side in a shout begins, 'The green eye of the Yellow God': and carries on unmoved through a dozen storm 'Binder' at him to the grave of mad Carew.

Second post trickles faintly through the steaming windows: then 'lights out,' short and sharp. With the switches' click comes darkness, surprising the late-sitters yet dressed on their beds. A snigger and two muttered curses from up the hut. Corporal Abner's voice rings loud, 'Silence there. I won't warn you again': and silence it is except for an intermittent whisper that might as well be the wind in a cracked window. I see the Corporal's cigarette doused: one more stone on the road to our earned unconsciousness of sleep. But hullo his bed's creaking! I raise my head and just get his whereabouts between me and a whited patch on the wall. Yes, he's sitting up. Now he has slid his legs quietly over the edge of the plaintive bed.

47

His trousers are still on. I rather feel than see him pad down the gangway past me. After whole minutes of dead silence in the hut the swish of slow feet creeps back over the linoleum, and a shadow re-crosses the light patch of wall. A blank run tonight. I extend my left arm and give 'all clear' to the next bed; he passes the signal on. The whispering of the cracked pane resumes.

The moon is a day past its full: and before midnight stands just at the level of the clerestory windows. Through their openness it shines squarely, very yellow and quiet, on my face: though little scurrying night-clouds flock ever about it, as if they begrudged us a full sight of their queen. Its rays fill the hut roof with shifting half-light, in which the piled kits on the long central shelf, with their flat caps atop, nod like drilled mandarins over the shadowed beds.

Everything new in this camp, animate or inanimate, must conform to the straight line that nature avoids and man fails to maintain. So the beams and ties of the roof-trusses are tonight futurist and mysterious, being pendent with all our equipment, slung up there to dry stiff, after scrubbing. The beds, of course, should now be drowning in silence, under the low breathing which is the brother of silence: but R.A.F. beds are so hard that every sleeper turns crampily about, once or twice in the hour, and groans as he turns: and so hot are our bellies that you will not wait three minutes in this hut of fifty-four men without hearing a loud spirtle of wind from some-one. 'The cry of an imprisoned turd,' they call it: our surest humour, which may break the tension even of an Armistice two minutes. The very sergeants shake with laughter when one leaps out roundly: for farts are not punishable like any other retort. Sailor can fart every five minutes, inimitably, with all the force and stink of nature. We expect the comment from him, whenever a senior is pompous.

11

FATIGUES

Fatigues, fatigues, fatigues. They break our spirits upon this drudgery. One of us ninety recruits (to so many are we grown) already wishes aloud he had not joined the R.A.F. In under a week we have clicked three or four fire-pickets ("Swinging it on the fucking rookies, they are, the old sweats,' grumbled Tug. 'Old soldier, old cunt,' quoted Madden with a laugh. 'Ah,' flung back Tug malevolently, 'young soldier, fly fucker. That's me'), dust-cart we get, and refuse-collection, scrubbing the shit-houses, the butcher's shop, the Q.M. Stores, Barrack Stores, sweeping and dusting the Cinema. Then there's message running at H.Q., the main point of which is to bring back for the clerks' elevenses their Chelsea buns while warm. China got into disgrace there. 'I wasn't going to fuck about for those toffee-nosed buggers, so I got back after fucking twelve, and they shoved me on the fizzer!'

He received two extra fatigues, as punishment:—which was getting off scot-free, for we are all, innocent and guilty, on extra fatigues, what with stoking the boiler-house or in the cook-house, or at the officers' mess, or hut cleaning or polishing the fire-station, or washing down the pigsties, or feeding the incinerator. At dawn we leap from bed, rush to wet our hands and faces, fall in for P.T.: fall out and fall in for breakfast, put on puttees and overalls, sweep the hut (under the eye of our corporal, who has us all by name, and misses nothing of what we fail to do), tidy our beds again, and fall in for fatigues. After that the hut does not see us, except for a hurried moment each side of dinner, till tea-time: and after tea is fire-picket, save for those who work an evening shift till nine at officers' mess, or dining hall, or civilian hut.

These two last are scullion jobs:—and not in neat sculleries with sinks and racks and hot taps. We dip into a tub of cold water, through its crusted grease, four or five hundred tea-stained mugs and a thousand plates: which afterwards we smooth over with a ball of grease-stiff rag. A stomach-turning smell and feel of muck it is, for hour upon hour: and a chill of water which shrivels our fingers. Then a clattered piling of wet dishes on the table, to drip dry. Nor may you ever call yourself your own, or a job yours. The camp pullulates with recruits, and every employed man's our master, who will get from us what privy convenience he can. Many exercise a spite upon the recruits so that out of fear we may be more accommodating. The Sergeant Major set an example of misuse, when he led the last fatigue man in the rank to his wife's house, and had him black the grate and mind the children, while she shopped. 'Gave me a slab of jam-tart, she did,' boasted Garner, lightly forgiving the crying infant because of the belly-full he'd won. We are always hungry.

The six-weeks men we meet on fatigues shock our moral sense by their easy-going. 'You're silly cunts, you rookies, to sweat yourselves,' they say. Is it our new keenness, or a relic of civility in us? For by the R.A.F. we shall be paid all the twenty-four hours a day, at three halfpence an hour; paid to work, paid to eat, paid to sleep: always those halfpence are adding up. Impossible, therefore, to dignify a job by doing it well. It must take as much time as it can for afterwards there is not a fireside waiting, but another job. The gods allow us in our hut just long enough to clean it, and our brass and leather and cloth—and they make the hut bare and regimental, so that we do not wish to linger in it. Our days pass half-choked in dusty offices, or menially in squalid kitchens, to and from which we hurry at a quick-step in fours through the verdant beauty of the park and its river valley: the stamp of our armoured feet fighting down the thrushes' twitter and the grave calling of rooks in the high elms.

12

REVEILLE

Our morning turn-out is sleepy. Few hear the long reveille floating through the camp in the black restlessness of nature before dawn. But Corporal Abner, old soldier and older man, has been stirring some while in the darkness, pulling on his clothes. With the first trumpet note he is stamping into his boots. 'Out now, lads,' he yells harshly, the long menace of him lunging at the switches down our aisle this side of the bar, and up the other. We roll over heavy with sleep and paw blindly for yesterday's socks by the bedside. If our noses were not as sleep-filled as our eyes we should easily find these socks, clotted as they are with the wear of several yesterdays.

However, we have them on at last and reluctantly we lower our legs over the bedside and grope them into the clammy trousers. Out of bed now: we tightly stuff in the ample shirt-tails, tie our braces round our waists, slip on shoes. We roll our mattresses and crown them with an ornamental sandwich of the layered blankets and sheets:—unless it's a Saturday, as today, when one clean sheet is issued each man in exchange for the more soiled of his pair. The first twenty minutes of morning pass in a constrained rush. Only those few loosen their voices who have run over to the wash-house for a sluice. One of these, today, against the hut's chilly discouragement tried to sing a verse of the sad little insect which had been his honey bee. But Dickson, with puckered painful forehead, begged him to put a sock in it. P.T., after a wet-bar night, is not a joke.

However, this morning we were lucky. Normally the early exercise is more torment than training; the pimple-faced Gym Instructors, beef-fed to bursting point with strutting muscles all alive oh, jangle us like frightened sheep round and round the square under the baleful eye of the crippled Commandant, till all are breathless and the faint-hearted fall out. Today our basilisk was absent and it was in free air that the chief instructor, a dapper sergeant, took us. He knew the real, not the showy exercises, and we deep-breathed and chest-expanded and at his word bent and twisted and turned, carefully but quickly. Before us on a high table he stood, his thin-vested body our exemplar. He did his own exercises, wholeheartedly, and when we followed well he smiled at us and cried, 'Good.'

The surprise of this, our first praise in the Depot, stiffened us so that we worked twice as hard, pumping ourselves dry with too-painstaking a copy of his movements. Seeing it he laughed and broke us into two bands which played tig and subdivided by trick orders, given to deceive us. So had done the other instructors: who when their tricks caught us would rave with anger against our crime. The sergeant laughed at his score off us when we miscarried and so heartened us to match ourselves against his next turn.

Half an hour passed in a long twinkling till the dismiss and the scurry back to the huts, where we fell on our beds to snatch wind. Our willingness had worked us out more than the daily fear: but the first use of our new breath was to make the long roof sound with praise of Sergeant Cunninghame. Only the unfit lay yet silent, panting through distressed mouths against

53

their load of strain. *Am I to class myself among these?* Till this year my insignificant body has met life's demands. If it fails me now I shall break it; but I hope it may scrape through. I try to excuse its inadequacy by remembering that I am eight years older than the next, and fifteen years older than many in the hut: but there is poor consolation in the first onset of age.

Yet today, despite my pumping chest, I managed the breakfast and was swaggering back from it when my eyes were held by the zinc roofs of the camp which slatted down the opposing slope of the valley from its tree-crest to the bank of the Pinne. The night-chill had beaded dew heavily upon them: and when the sun topped the ridge and vibrated between the fringing trees along the flat angle of the roofs, it silvered their wet steps into a cascade. Just for two minutes M. Section was very beautiful.

The half-hour after breakfast belongs to cleaning and tidying and is consecrated to song. Fifty of the fifty-four men in the hut chant continuously, each his fancied tune. Yet it might easily be worse: for there are no more than three songs in great vogue and their airs are short. 'Peggy O'Neil,' 'Sally,' 'The Beautiful City of Tears'; sentimental, sobbing things, whose dear girls die or go away for ever. If Sailor or Dickson begins such a song generally it will dominate, for there is an infective loveliness in the voices of these two men. The others then play their helpful parts whether in unison or in variety: the floor-broom sweeps, the boot-brushes brush, even the polishing rag polishes to and fro, in time with the choiring air. For the moment our hut and all of us thrum to a collective rhythm.

13

VANITIES

Our fatigue today was as fortunate as our P.T. Saturday is only a morning, and we were set to sweep and dust the Cinema after the Friday night of its glory, which had left the airmen's seats husky with nut-shells and toffee-wrappings and the officers' boxes floored with the silver foil of cigarettes and chocolate. Plain housemaiding seemed fun after our degraded week. So we made a song of it, so loud a song that the Second Sergeant Major, a great but mild star, looked in at the door and asked what we thought we were: the next glee-party, or fatigue men?

Snaggletooth, who was nearest the door (an older fellow, dark-faced, soldierly), gave him a pert answer not knowing him against the light. 'Christ,' he called to us after, 'I didn't half drop a bollock then. It was old man Jim himself.' 'Yes,' called back the little S.M. who had left the first door only to peep in at the second, 'and' (coming nearer) 'Jim's going to be very rude to you, my lad. I'm going to call you *Beaver.*' The laugh was on Snaggle, whose chin was indeed black. The sunlight capped our happiness. Was it not Saturday, a half-day: and Sunday, all day, tomorrow?

Good news in the hut, at noon. The tailors had taken pity on our imprisonment, and sent up the breeches and tunics for us all. These rawly blue clothes, littering the brown beds, lent to our mustard-coloured crowd something of the brightness of the summer's sky, outside, upon this noble day. Likewise they promised us the freedom of the gate. Few of us had served before, or experienced servitude. So we lusted for the wideness of the civilian world and burst out towards excess like escaped starlings. Some fellows picked up their 'bits of skin' even at the camp gates, by virtue of the rude maleness which is the service-man's repute.

But first there was a mass trying on and innocent vanity of the new dress, which was to be our best for the next years. If we were not just right the scrutiny of the sentry might know us for recruits, and the guard-corporal come: and then we'd be in trouble. With such a cloak of care for R.A.F. smartness did we hide our curiosity, competition, and desire to look well in the sight of 'birds.' These boys, in fancy dress for the first time, went stroking and smoothing their thighs, to make the wings of the breeches stand out richly. The tailors had taken them in at the knees, by our secret request, so tightly that they gripped the flesh and had a riding cut. Dandies put a wire in the outer seams to spread them more tautly sideways. Posh, that is.

Each dressed fellow blushingly accosted his half-section (so ruddy by contrast the high collar and pulled down peak made the familiar face) and said, 'How's this tunic? Are my cap, breeches, puttees right?' Corporal Abner, pestered too much, rose, reached for his cap and lounged slowly through the door, smiling always, gravely. Groups swarmed about the communal mirrors each end of the hut, enjoying the set of their breasts and pockets. It was nearly an hour before the last had trickled out to the open air and left me the hut and mirrors for my own.

These clothes are too tight. At every pace they catch us in a dozen joints of the body, and remind us of it. The harsh friction of the cloth excitingly polishes our skins and signals to our carnality the flexure of each developing muscle or sinew. They provoke lasciviousness, by telling so much of ourselves. Airmen cannot swing along like civvies, unconscious of their envelope of flesh. For them there is a sealed pattern of carriage, of the head, the trunk, the feet, the arms, the hands, the stick.

God's curse on that stick! A slip of black cane with a silver knob. I'd as soon dandle a doll through the street. We were ordered to hold it in the right hand, between thumb and second finger, at the point of balance, ferrule forward, sawing the fingers loosely and easily across it as we walked, so that the stick stayed always parallel with the ground, while the hands swung back and forward, to the height of the belt-line in front and rear at each stride, not bending the elbow, the hand going back as the foot went forward. *Try it, someone!* and remember that fear is with us when we break this rule. Any N.C.O. or officer, whether in uniform or plain clothes, if he see an irregularity has upon him the duty of taking our names. That the decent ones ignore this duty is to discipline's hurt and does not greatly help us: for every R.A.F. station has its pariahs, its service police, whose commendations are for reporting such minutiae of offence.

14

HOLIDAY

The rare privilege of a half-day made me anxious lest I miss some shred of its enjoyment. I wandered again into the park, to feel its decaying beauty: but achieved less keenly. My new kinship with the uniformed inhabitants bent my eye to draw longer pleasure from the blueness of a knot of fellows asprawl, gambling, in the grass, than from the greenness of the wild grass itself. I peeped to see if their breeches were shaped the way of ours: and my attuned ear found their gleeful ribaldry more apt than the chirping of the birds.

Tea-time and I cut it, luxuriously making the trumpet sound after me in vain. Our ration meals were plentiful, business-like, unappetising, because of their sameness in look and taste. So a yearning for the liberty of unofficial food conquered me. In my pocket rested a week's pay. I would visit the canteen and please myself.

Already, the days so drew in that they had turned on the lights: and the long wall of windows, which was the canteen, seemed brilliant across the dusk. In the small wet bar were a dozen airmen, cosily drinking. Only a dozen. The Air Force off duty craves food, not drink.

I passed to the entry of the dry-bar and pushed through its
thin door where the loose-hung latch clashed behind me twice

or thrice with the nervous haste of indecision. After all the huge room was not brightly lit. Behind the counter that ran athwart the near end stood a row of girls in uniform, to serve. Across the far side stretched a file of billiard tables upon whose green flats stood cones of yellow light from shaded overhanging globes. Dull-clothed men were moving restlessly around the tables, to the click of balls. As they leaned forward to play, their buttons glittered and the lamp-glare detached their white faces as so many masks against the shadowed walls. The sharp tread of nailed ammunition boots on the linoleum, or the sibilant shuffle of rubber gymnasium shoes came obscurely from the half-light. These and a chink of thick cups on thick saucers were thrown up like castanets, shakily, over an undertone of humming conversation.

I took place by the counter in the queue: among a continual come and go of men, in whose faces despite their common, airmanly likeness (the professional mark, general even here, off duty, in our own house, unfixed) shone a new alertness, a mobility of eye and interest in the matter in hand: which was generally food. Tea and wads, sausages and mashed. Are they able always to eat?

I can, anyway. The girl in blue overalls handed me a filled plate with the smile and gay word which was the fleeting routine of these hard-pressed servers. It was cheap food and plain to bareness: but not worse than most of our lives' habit. The mere exercise of choice is the attraction. The voluntary faculty atrophies in service life except we buy here from our own pockets much what the 'mess-deck' would give us freely. Yet slop tea tastes better from a cup than from a mug, and so on.

For me there promised, also, the rarity of an independent table; one of that colony of four-seater tables which chequered the middle of the room. Their cotton cloths were splotched   59 with food stains, gravelled with old crumbs, and blocked with the used plates and cups of my forerunners. No matter: at least half of them were free. I shouldered open a clearing for my load, and sat down to taste a lonely pleasure after two weeks of the crowd. I had taken on this effort partly to replace myself in a world from which much solitary thinking had estranged me: just now I was feeling the first, worst, strain of it: a short interlude of dreamy quiet would be refreshment, not recreance.

Round the walls hung tinted photographs of King George, Trenchard, Beatty, Haig, some land-girls, a destroyer at speed. Even there was a small picture of me, a thing later conveyed slyly to the ever-open incinerator. The gloom-shrouded trusses of the distant roof fluttered restlessly with other dusty relics of war-time: cotton flags of the late allies. Behind my back a piano struck up. It hesitated on certain notes, and the listening at stretch while my imperfect ear tried to pick out which notes these were, had the effect of waking me again before I had properly lost myself. For the matter of that the keynote of the great hall was restlessness. In ten minutes I was sauntering up and down it, like the others, in the grip of their contagious not-knowing-what-to-do.

Some had met the problem, temporarily, by starting a dance on the bit of floor by the piano: dancing to the tune of anything, played oddly anyhow by a man in blue. He was not expert and the piano's wires had gone slack with over-hammering. Surely there was something sorry in the sight of those twenty couples of men circling together? They would be womanless now, most of them, for seven years. Their faces were grim. To them dancing was a rite; and the confined floor to their taste. They gladdened themselves in the press when they bumped together—so solemnly. There was no public

60

laughter here or anywhere in the hall: no raised voices in its ebb and flow; only gentleness to one another and a returned gentleness to the quick-eyed serving-women. We receive the rough tongue from sergeants and corporals all the day-time: and the first smart of that makes us glad to extend a public gentleness, ourselves, whenever it is permitted.

The night was turning to mist: and our hut was yet empty. So early a return was not in order for a holiday. But the hut was now my friendly familiar place and my bed in it a home. There the quietness which had eluded me in the canteen waited or returned, as I lay remembering with shame my panic at this hour of my first night in the Depot when I was so fearful of what the other fellows might do to me. Shyness with men was now and for ever overpast after fourteen days, only; long days: but my soul, always looking for some fear to salt its existence, was wondering what seven whole years of servitude would do against the hasty stubbornness which had hitherto buttressed my values. The question took a self-pitiful turn, and I mizzled gently in the white-walled silence, to the minor accompaniment of the cinema orchestra refined into faintness by passage through two buildings and across a hundred yards of air. *Surely it must have begun to rain?* That trumpet call had an almost liquid beauty.

The others began to come in from the streets. Animal heat steamed from the dampness of their clothes, with the sweetly-cloying smell of a sheep-pen some October evening. The hairs of their tunics' curling nap were spangled with the first drops of the night's rain. Late-comers were sodden to blackness. Airmen's knees get wet, first, because the edges of our over-coats conduct the drip thither: and the strained cloth over the joint laps up the water in a moment. Life is hard for service men whose spare-clothes are wet through. We have no drying fires: and by day everything, wet or dry, must be folded away to pattern. So it may take a week of night-airing to get them right.

Cook, the ex-seaman, staggered through the door. At once his pals took charge. One hasted to put down his bed while another stretched him on the hut form and stripped him. Together they tucked him up: in turn they held his basin while he vomited. Some laughed at his plight, but the seniors checked them, saying, 'Poor bugger: he's properly loaded.' The sense was that one of us had met misfortune. James, our young and very proud acetylene-welder, sneered with the uncharity of the not-yet-fallen. 'Cunt shouldn't bastard-well drink if he can't carry it.' 'Wait,' said Peters angrily, 'till you grow up and a man offers you a wet.'

As I lay dozing, snatches of these Saturday conversations shouted through the din on three sides of my lying-place assaulted my ears. 'Jock had a pot tonight in the wet canteen.' 'Bollocks: the barman only shook his bloody apron at him, and he went arse-ways on the fucking floor.' 'They do the hesitation and the chain in the same movement.' 'Golly, I didn't half want it: she fair lifted.' 'He swore he'd been on sherry and bitters all fucking night, and it was only bastard-well twenty-past six, and the bloody bar hadn't opened till six.' 'Her eyes were starey, like a haddock's: gave my fucking arsehole a headache.' 'The poshest guy had white shoes, and white flannel slacks, and his blue tunic. Boy, he looked bloody smart.' 'If we're daft they're fucking lunatics at Rugby.' 'What about the brooches lost? The M.C. calls Silence, any Lady lost a brooch. See all the tarts grab their tits.' 'Stoke's famous for cracked pots.' 'Anyway, it doesn't take six cunting towns to make our burg.' 'One snaky piece had a low dress, and she shimmied.'

A fescennine court-martial, some beds off, woke all to full attention, it was so loud. Sailor's rich voice, beer-polished, rose and fell across China's snarl. Lofty was being charged with blanket-drill. 'Swinging the dolphin,' Sailor called it with a lapse into seafaring. Corporal Abner moved up two beds to interfere if the parties fell to demonstration: but it ended in alcoholic laughter, by good hap. Drunkenness sometimes unbridles the flesh, as nightmare hounds out the brain.

Without in the darkness the rain affirmed itself. Closer columns of raindrops bore down on the supine earth and drove all life to cover. Lights out came at last, to my craving ear. Silence wiped out their horrid babel and let the rain-sound, already ruling the outer air, win the dark hut and rule it too. There was no moon, only a road-lamp glimmering through the windows to pencil edges of light along the roof-beams and their gallows of rafters, overhead. Very deep in the night I woke again, because a squall lashed our windows. Its wind had cleared half the sky and betrayed the moon's disc wobbling in the wet-filmed panes.

15

CHURCH

After Saturday night—Sunday. Only a service-man can hear the sighing content of that 'Sunday.' Airmen fall asleep the night before in inexhaustible wealth of leisure. Even, perhaps, we might lie in, tomorrow morning. But with the daylight some of the glamour had gone. Our blue clothes make us available for Church, and Church Parade is reputed the fiercest inspection of the week. At this Depot they also train officers in their duties. Do we not hear Stiffy, the fat drill-adjutant and ringmaster of our circus, telling them off before the filled parade-ground for faults of carriage or command? Does he not on Sundays allot to each a special examination? One to find so many dull boots; another to report men whose cap-badges are too high or too low (in our three weeks we have twice had to change our badges by order), another to scrutinise chins, and take the names of those which are stubbly. Training for them, punishment for us. Easy to avoid, that last crime? Not if your shaving has been in an unlit windy wash-house, mirrorless, with cold water at six in the morning while a dozen chaps shove for your place by the tap.

Because of such forebodings the reality of the parade seemed light. It rained so we belted the looseness of our great-coats round us, bayonets weighing down our left haunches (bayonets are essential for divine service), and the silly bodkin-sticks in our right hands. Many of us had never before done a church parade. We were shuffled into sections temporarily called 'flights' and marched down High Street, our iron-clad boots shambling, sliding and clinking on the muddied setts. No one could wish to keep step. The officers were new to us and shy of raising their voices in public, above the band and the clatter of traffic and the blanketing rain. Orders came down the files by word of mouth. The being conducted like cattle to market as a show between staring pavements was rarely horrible.

The much-restored fourteenth-century church was three parts full of our blue waves, on which the oddly-mobile heads rolled loosely, above the pew-backs. Mobile heads, for eyes were no longer chained to the front, and odd heads, in colour and shape: for all caps were off, a betrayal which never happened by day except as now, in church. Recruit-heads were clipped to the blood and pale as the scalp's pink. Even senior men were compelled to have pigs' bristles, like ours, at the neck: but on top their hair was very long, and greased tightly to their skulls, so as to fit inconspicuously under their caps. Airmen will risk any punishment rather than go cropped like soldiers. We claim warrant: are we not the *'air* force?

To the clerics we should have looked promising listeners, because our rain-reddened ears stuck out very large and free below the furrow bitten into the scalp by the tight cap-band. But also bullet-heads and stuff-collared necks show a brutality which seems to scare men of God. Most of them take so for granted in their every word that we are particular sinners.

He was a feeble, throaty parson whose bookish face faded when our phalanx solidly sang the first hymn. *Early in the morning my song shall rise to thee.* Too early, our rising this   65

morning. Reveille as usual: the weather a murky drizzle: no
P.T.: breakfast an hour late. We had to loaf that hour, un-
naturally, deflating our windy stomachs in wordless silence.
The chanties which ordinarily made rhythmical the hour of
kit-cleaning and sweeping hut were today chilled on our lips.
Some did not even sweep up.

From the pew behind me rang out the rich Tyneside voice of
Sailor, now casting down his golden crown about the glassy sea
as gustily as yesterday he'd sung:

*'The first to come was the Bosun's wife, and she was dressed in
blue,*

And in one corner of her cunt, she'd stowed the cutter's crew!

*She stowed the cutter's crew, my boys, the rowlocks and the
oars,*

And in the other corner, was the Air Force forming fours,

    Singing "Wack ja, the do ra-lay."

    Her hair hung down from her cunt, Sir,

    For

     She

      Was

       One

    Of the good old Pompey whores!

*'The next to come was the Gunner's wife, and she was dressed
in russet,*

And in one corner of her cunt, she stowed a twelve-inch turret!

*She stowed those twelve-inch guns, my boys, also the shot and
the shell,*

And in the other corner, were the turret's crew as well!

*'The next to come was the Captain's wife, and she was dressed
in black,*

And in one corner of her cunt, . . .'

The chuckle even now latent in Sailor's throat gave me a smiling picture of the confusion of dinted crowns in Heaven, when the saints had been dismissed off casting drill.

We sat to pray, and the emanations of wet wool and sweat gathered over us. Surely we were steeped in flesh. Before me stood the font, from whose quatrefoil panel into my face leered a mediaeval face, with ringed mouth and protruding tongue. Its lewdness somehow matched our prison-coloured lolling heads: while the padre read a lesson from Saint Paul, prating of the clash of flesh and spirit and of our duty to fight the body's manifold sins. The catalogue of these sins roused us to tick off on grubby fingers what novelties were left us to explore. For the rest we were just uncomprehending. Our ranks were too healthy to catch this diseased Greek antithesis of flesh and spirit. Unquestioned life is a harmony, though then not in the least Christian.

More relieving hymns, and then a sermon on prayer: the ejaculations, he said, of the soul in ecstasy labouring through joy and sorrow after God. Not half. I remembered Cook last night stumbling to a fall over the foot of my bed, and how he'd chokingly prayed 'God fuck me' thrice to the giggling hut. So do we pray. The padre, ignoring our life, ignored equally our language. Spiritually we were deaf one to the other: while around and over us flowed the exquisite cadences of the Tudor service-book: a prose too good for him and too good for us. Generations ago the poor were brought up on Bible and prayer-book, and used such golden rhythms in their speech. Now for everyday they have a choppy prose, like rag-time; and for moments of emotion the melodrama of film-captions. To my ears these sound strained and literary: but they have soaked them to the bones in years of picture-going.

At last we were through with it and passing swiftly home-   67 ward up the street to the square, ready for dismissal. Alas, a shock awaited us. There stood the broken scowling Commandant, of whose guts good words might be spoken, reluctantly: but who had no humanity in him towards airmen. He ordered that our parade march past him in slow time. No officer dared speak to him, uninvited: so not even stout Stiffy could tell him we were in part unsquadded recruits, whose drills had not begun. The first ranks, older airmen, led the movement. Each flight behind copied the flight ahead: so the pattern quickly deteriorated. The officers did not know what orders to give. Flight tangled with flight, in line, in column, cross-wise. Some dressed right, some left. The flight commanders, not able to determine which was the directing flank, doubled imitatively this side and that like hares.

Our lot were certainly too forward: someone turned us about, marched us back and let us march, till we burst into the ranks of Flight 9. Our proper officer had a piping voice; so inevitably our distant men obeyed the roaring officer of the flight in rear. Suddenly we formed two deep: wrong: we had to be foured, and wheeled again. What we were doing the others were doing, busily. The press got so tight that we could move only pace by pace. The band's spirited conductor rose to the occasion with Chopin's funeral march. The 'Saul' would have been better, but to play it without a funeral is a service offence. The same judgment makes a crime of repeating 'Tommy here and Tommy there' in barracks.

The Commandant was beaten. With a wave of the arm he gave the maelstrom to Stiffy, limped to his car, and went. Over our heads rang out in the hugest voice of my life, Stiffy's shout, 'Royal Air Force: on your huts: MOVE.' It was the dismissal from P.T. 'When I say MOVE,' Sergeant Cunninghame had taught us, 'your feet don't touch the ground. You fly.' So the mob scattered as if high explosive had been fired in its heart, and after a minute the square was empty, but the huts volleying with laughter.

Only our Peters, the tall and soldierlike, who had been picked to hold the colours behind the Commandant was angry. 'The biggest balls-up ever. Stiffy was laughing like a cunt. If my old mob had seen it they'd have dropped dead. I've lost my last respect for the Air Force. The bloody colours were only a rag on a stick. Ours were silk, with honours. There isn't a spot of what they call "whores de combatte" about this crowd.'

Peters stood a little outside our ranks. His perfection of drill, and soldiering experience (fruits of a hidden two years in the Line), made him conceited with the picture of his grace standing out against our ungainliness. Also he got a parcel once— something to eat—and kept it to himself. Who could trust him, after that?

Corporal Abner warned us the orderly sergeant was prowling the huts to find men for fire-picket. So we nipped through the back door of our hut (which gave on to the grass) and across to the scruffy, friendly Y.M. There we sat and talked and laughed and drank tea and ate wads, awaiting dinner.

16

MESS DECK

The dining hall (Mess Deck in our tongue) was a vast cross-headed hall, with floor of resonant cement, about which the iron-legged forms and tables were dragged with a sound of thunder. Din filled its walls at meal-times, when we packed in, twelve a table, all talking deeply through food-thickened throats. Din of the iron food-trays: din of those who wielded the heavy serving-spoons. The last two comers to each table have to fetch the grub from the kitchen (in a bay off the central limb) and dish it out. So tables are filled at the run, men jostling each other to avoid the invidious last seats. Their boot-nails scream like tearing silk on the swilled floor: a sharp sound which went well with the occasional sharpness of knife or fork against a plate.

Across this body of noise would cut the sudden whistle of the orderly sergeant, to introduce the officer of the day. If these were decent fellows they came in hat in hand: if old soldiers, they swaggered through as in a street. At each table when they passed, the end man would jerk to his feet, bark 'No complaints Sir,' and drop like a shot rabbit. He could not stand longer for the form cut into the back of his knees: so a bobbing undulation and staccato fire of words marked their progress. There were never complaints: we might be recruits but we knew that first law of safety. Just the fast work with knife, fork and spoon went on till the plateful was finished and a swill of water from one of the table's four mugs washed it down. Meat came in one tin, vegetables in the second: and often pudding in a third.

The division was as fair as haste and amateur judgment allowed: though a recording angel, taking down our talk, would not have thought it. We pretend to the lowest opinion of our betters' honesty. If margarine is short, it is the cook who has pinched it, or the Air Ministry is saving on our rations. Biscuits (not eatable biscuits, but the iron ration) are issued in place of bread for Friday's tea:—because we are paid on Friday, and the Air Ministry wants our hunger to give the canteen first pick of our pockets.

We soon grumble at the food, and grow tired of it. If we have any money we are likely to reject it queasily, and go buy much the same stuff in the canteen. The atmosphere of Mess Deck was against any estimation of its meals, and forbade the entertainment of any flavour but its own. To enter the echoing place between meals was repellent. The dank gloom so caught throat and nose with its reminder of cooked meat.

Sometimes the Powers, suspecting monotony in our diet, order the cooks to create a novelty. God save His airmen! Tinned salmon and fried onions they gave us for breakfast once. 'Hell,' shouted China. 'Next it'll be winkles and fucking watercress.' Again:—'Chips for dinner: fuck 'em,' said Hoxton in disgust. He had always eaten his chips of an evening, with fish, from a stall. Your workman dislikes the untried. Yet at the end of dinner Hoxton wiped his mouth with a 'Well, that wasn't too bad,' the services' highest word of praise. Stomachs agree upon only one point: that bacon and eggs make the world's richest breakfast. Give to a table twelve spindly brine-sodden rashers, and a tin of stale eggs noisomely splattered in the grease which a half-hour ago had been frying fat—and twelve men will roll out of Mess Deck, ripe-feeling and full, with praise of the messing officer. 'Bon' are bacon and eggs.

17

CORPORAL ABNER

After Sunday dinner, for some, a sleep. That's the worst of living in a bedroom with only beds to rest on. 'Off duty into kip,' says the old sweat, that contemptible type of routine-sodden brain. Not that any of us try to bulge with mind. Many airmen have had schooling and have been curious. Thus Horder, two days back, borrowed my Laforgue and has been chuckling slyly over its recondite humours: but happiness in the service and (still more important) good-fellowship jointly entail our living on the surface.

There lies a golden mist of laughter—even if silly laughter—over our hut. Shake together fifty-odd fellows, strangers of every class, in a close room for twenty days: subject them to a new and arbitrary discipline: weary them with dirty, senseless, uncalled for yet arduous fatigues . . . but there has not been a sharp word between any two of us. Such liberality of body and spirit, such active vigour, cleanliness and good temper would hardly have persisted save in the conditions of a common servitude.

More and more I feel that the hut receives its serenity from our corporal, who has personality to lend out. The grave brooding of the man has grown dominant. At first he was gentle, admonitory, perhaps father-like. With time he tightened: and our younger fellows resenting (or wishing to taste?) the bit, danced angrily. We have been led here by our innate impulses and are offering the R.A.F. our best. So the curtness of command and its professional severities jar on us. The spur would feel more earned towards the end of the stage. Yet I suspect Corporal Abner is right to harden us early. So large a service cannot be all good. We are its ridden beasts; and of our officers and N.C.O.s some will be bad riders. We must acquire the stolidity to carry on and like the work too well to let it suffer, however they mishandle or punish us, ignorantly. The R.A.F. is bigger than itself.

Abner showed himself very much of a man: but always he was a little sad and quiet. I, hating noise, was grateful that he did not bark like an imitation sergeant major; I suspected him of resenting much that he had to make us undergo, and of seeing the futility of most routine. Routine is too often an easy way of saving thought. Also he bore the Powers' abuse for our shortcomings. We could not be well tutored, because we were scattered, day long, on fatigues. We were too raw to group ourselves, too independent to ask humbly, too ignorant to know what we had to learn. We were more than content, indeed proud, if we scraped through the day unhurt.

So Abner could not hope to achieve great things with us. He was courteous to sincere enquiry, sardonic towards the thoughtless, brusque with the shy. He exacted quick obedience to any order (when at last he drove himself to give one) and threatened the slack. The rebellious? Not yet; we had joined to serve: but many did not care enough about his trifles, and were still lively. At last, after five weeks' patience, he denounced fourteen of us to the Sergeant Major, for untidy kit. The punishment was an extra fire-picket each: a trifle, and he had long endured: but they hated him for it.

74

Had he been humorous or lewd we should have borne him better. But Abner was ever serious. 'Who's this fellow with no boots by his bed?' was his complaint one morning. When he recognised his own bed he only passed on, grimly. Hard, no doubt, for an oldish man to lodge, week after week, in a monkey house like ours. He had no conversation for us, but one afternoon two friends came for him and he took them to the canteen and entertained them till closing time. Rumour makes him roaring drunk last year at Hendon, on Display night, while he oversaw the clearing of the refreshment tents. We hope so, and repeat the tale to convince ourselves.

Abner was strong-faced with a hollow jaw like a tank, level brows and a broad low forehead. His regard was direct and disconcerting for his eyes were curiously deep and his lower jaw—that very heavy lower jaw—dropped a little. So his parted lips seemed ready either to smile or to speak. It gave him a deliberate air: but always his word was grave and I suspected always pity in his smile.

He was an artist in soldiering, in dress, in kit-folding. None of us could in half an hour equal the bed he squared in three minutes. Yet everywhere was this puritan avoidance of display. Almost he seemed ashamed of being smart. Later, when we had left the Depot, we found this was the mark of the real airman as distinguished from the 'Stiffy pet.' Meanwhile he puzzled us. Of course he was old. In the war he had been an army signaller. He had earned three wound-stripes, and handled our noise as if we could never be things to be afraid of. Only he had too little laughter. Yet, on parade, he would be evidently laughing in his eyes as he poised himself to face us, rocking back a little on his heels to cry an order. What was it so amused him, then?

18

BAKER'S ROLL-CALL

Tonight's crash of the stick on the hut door at roll-call was terrific; and the door slammed back nearly off its hinges. Into the light strode Baker, V.C., a corporal who assumed great licence in the camp because of his war-decoration. He marched down my side of the hut, checking the beds. Little Nobby, taken by surprise, had one boot on and another off. Corporal Baker stopped. 'What's the matter with YOU?' 'I was knocking out a nail which hurts my foot.' 'Put your boot on at once. Your name?' He passed on to the end door and there whirled round, snorting, 'Clarke.' Nobby properly cried, 'Corporal,' and limped down the alley at a run (we must always run when called) to bring up stiffly at attention before him. A pause, and then curtly, 'Get back to your bed.'

Still the Corporal waited and so must we, lined up by our beds. Again, sharply, 'Clarke.' The performance was repeated, over and over, while the four files of us looked on, bound fast by shame and discipline. We were men, and a man over there was degrading himself and his species, in degrading another. Baker was lusting for trouble and hoped to provoke one of us into some act or word on which to base a charge. Nobby limped submissively up and down perhaps eight times, before the other door admitted Corporal Abner. Baker wheeled and vanished.

When Abner heard our story he went out of the hut again and came back just before lights out, smiling grimly.

A private affair lightened the hour for me. Day by day I had been putting down these notes on our Depot life, often writing in bed from roll-call till lights out, using any scrap of paper. So I seemed only to be writing letters. They were now grown to an unmanageable crumpled bulk. Yet I could not send the earlier ones away, for often I went back with fuller understanding to a past experience and implemented it; or ran the collected impressions of, say, three fire-pickets into one. At last there came to my memory a loose-leaf notebook, blank, among my papers in London; and I wrote for it. It had come today and I now unpacked it to begin transcribing: but as I gave the pages a preliminary shake, there dropped out on the floor my parchment patent of long ago, as Minister Plenipotentiary:— 'George' you know 'to his Trusty and Well-beloved' . . . with a seal on it as red and nearly as broad as my face. 'What's that?' asked Peters, the inquisitive. 'My birth-certificate,' I said glibly, shovelling it out of sight.

19

SHIT-CART

At eight in the morning four of us stood about the Transport Yard feeling out of sorts with life. Just our luck to have clicked 'shit-cart' on a Monday, the double-load day. Our scruffy driver (all 'Drivers Pet.' in the R.A.F. are scruffy) tickled his bus, and struggled to swing her coldly-sluggish engine. At last she roared off. We flung ourselves at her flying tail-board and clambered in. The lorry turned left, down over the bridge. To M. Section, evidently. Hillingdon House looked forlorn, because of its black windows, behind whose wideness the clerks lounged with their first cups of tea. 'Jammy cunts,' sneered Sailor enviously. Clerks hadn't to get up at six. Our hands were cold and the lorry's dirty body jigged rattlingly over the rough road.

M. Section cook-house. 'Two of you to each,' ordered the Corporal. We lifted the tall galvanised-iron bins and staggered with them along the beset kitchen area up the muddy cement steps to the road. There we joined forces, three heaving up the bins while the other, in the lorry, pulled from above. Twenty-six bins, say two tons. A lot of kitchen spoil for eight hundred men? Yes, but each service throws away enough food to feed the other two.

Some of Saturday's bins were packed hard with the settling

of their own weight of soot, bones, paper, broken food, plates and glass, hundreds of tins, rotting meat and straw, old clothes: and mouldy green bread which smelt like coconut. Someone had poured gallons of black stuff, like treacle, on the top: and this had cemented even ash and potato peelings into one tight pudding. Four bins refused to tip out: we had to spoon their contents forth with our hands. It was not so bad to the touch, but a shivery sight to see a clean arm go into it: and hard to know how to hold the polluted limb afterwards.

The lorry was half-filled. Up we went in her again. Now we were not tossed about, after she started. The enchaining muck was much over our knees. As the speed increased, the lorry's jerking riddled the load. What was wet and heavy silted to the floor: while the dust and ashes rose to the top. Even they rose beyond the top, in a haze which slowly thickened as the road ran away behind us. To save Camp from the infection of blown filth, Authority had tented over the refuse wagon with a tarpaulin tilt, and prescribed that the back curtain must be kept tightly down. Our today's fatigue corporal was a literalist, so we obeyed literally. Yet the refuse uttered a choke like fire-damp. We four inside passengers stumbled to the tail, and thrust our gasping heads through the crack of the back curtain. By craning round the side of the bus we could get our mouths full of the blessed wind made by our passage at speed up the rising road.

Here's the officers' cook-house. Five bins: cushy: though after forty lifts and carries the single bin feels not so light as it did. On again the few score yards to our cook-house. Plenty more bins: but, thank Heaven, level ground. The thin handles have cut and blistered our finger joints, and our forearms ache with lifting these tons of muck. Also something, probably the reek within the lorry, has cut short our breath at the root. **79**

'Double up with those last bins,' cried the Corporal, who knew it was only a few minutes to dinner-time. 'Double up, yourself,' growled Boyne, angry like the rest of us and feeling the full severity of each lift, now, as only a dispirited man can feel long work and the loss of his dinner. I was trying not to laugh at the other three. The ashes sifting into their eyebrows and down their sweaty cheeks had made such smooth old men of them. And of me doubtless, had I seen myself.

Up, down: up, down. A long walk back with the light bin; and a stagger out again with a full one. Up, down: up, down: up, down. The maddening repetition is over. Boyne lends us his hand from above, and we pull ourselves stiffly up the high tail-board. None of this morning's monkey-jumping, now. Down with the curtain again, I suppose. We are buried much more than thigh-deep. As the lorry lurches round corners we sprawl into it helplessly, coughing and spitting. My overall-legs are getting stuffed from the bottom with ordures of sorts. Something bubbly and soft is working up into my crotch. Too smooth for a rat, anyway. We are running fast, just here, down the long stretch to the incinerator. Hurrah, we've passed the canteen and may lift the curtain. Nobody to report us on this road at dinner-time. Clean air began to filter in as the dust and ashes streamed out.

The driver pulled up at the incinerator and we got down to cough and gasp the red back to our faces. 'Back her in and drop the tail-board,' saith the Corporal. But the driver is an old sweat, not a rookie's easy meat. 'Will I fuck! Think I'm on bastard heat? She'll stay as she fuckin' well is till I've had me bleedin' conner.' 'Fall in, you four,' barked the Corporal at us, harshly, to cover his discomfiture: and he marched us stiffly back to cook-house, calling left, right, left-right-left, to draw attention to his regimentality. The squads were just going on for their afternoon drill: we blushed they should see our drudgery. The being marched before onlookers, unnecessarily, humiliates troops more than anything. It rubs in their bondage.

The cook had not kept any dinners: but after a grumble he produced a pan of broken stuff. As the Corporal did not let us fall out for a wash we could not pretend annoyance when they judged us too smelly for the dining hall. So we wolfed our grub, standing, in a corner of the scullery passage, off the lime-washed lids of the bins we'd emptied. Fifteen minutes later we were marching back. Left-right, left-right. Damn the fool.

Now it was spade-work. We had to shovel our load into the hopper of the incinerator. Back-breaking exercise for tired or sorry men. More blisters: months since we had shovelled any-thing. 'Why O why did I join the Air Force?' comically grieved little Nobby, a weakling whose inclusion in today's party has thrown extra work on Boyne, Sailor the cheery, and myself. Our corporal was driving us hard. After the refuse we should have to fetch the swill, which many called the worst of the job.

We ground back, up the gradient. M. Section's swill (the emptyings of every man's plate, and all wet objects of food judged fit for the camp pigs) filled eleven bins. We loaded them complete into our lorry. They weighed heavier than the rubbish, for every one brimmed with gallons of sour milk. This wasted cow-juice soured us too: camp tea was so bitterly under-milked.

Whenever the lorry jumped a pot-hole the bins erupted over us in great gouts. A stale-smelling bath. Here and there in the camp we found more stuff to pick up: the hospital was throwing much away. Then at last down the park road to the pigsties, whose population squealed us a delighted welcome as their great moment of the day arrived. We poured out grey lakes into each trough and they bathed in it.

Our day seemed finished. The Corporal gave us a breather in

81

the golden sunset, saying, 'Half-past four: pretty good for a Monday.' We failed to glow with his praise. He had not lent us a hand's turn all day. In this he had the letter of regulations on his side: but there were few corporals poor enough to put the letter before the job.

One of our hut fellows had flung me a letter, last time we pounded down the road. I now fished it from the pouch of my swill-stinking stiffened overalls. The splashes we had caught in the lorry were soaking coldly through our shirts, making our skins tacky like perished rubber. The letter too was soaked, and its envelope shredded open in my raw hand. I read with smarting eyes the offer of a friendly publisher to give me the editorship of his projected highbrow monthly 'Belles-lettres.' I stared from the lovely clouds to my foul clothes, and wondered how it would feel to go back.

We imagined we were resting the last moments of the working day so as to return dutifully late to the orderly room for 'dismiss.' But suddenly the Corporal called us to fall in again. 'Cunt thinks he's drilling the fucking depot,' snarled Nobby, beside his thin soul with rage at this pretence to ceremonialise a job of scavenging. 'Get those forks, and shift the pig-shit into the lorry.' 'Want to make yourself a nice bed, Corp?' questioned Sailor blandly.

We felt like murder. Was the show never going to end? We had done nine hours of it already. I could feel the reality of my own aches: if the others were as bad, then we were a sorry crew. Only I dared not, with my pound-note accent, fall down and fail in a job. They'd have taken for granted I was too soft for man's work. So I lifted the great fork and tried to pick up the stringy dirt. At last it was all in. The lorry moved over to the garden, where was a manure heap: painfully we added our share to the pile. This did end the fatigue. 'You can ride back,' offered the Corporal. Boyne and I jumped out. Not for us one voluntary minute of the uncleanly stench which had poisoned us all day.

At the hut, near six o'clock (no tea for us, of course) we too hastened to wash. The ashes had caked with sweat into every wrinkle of our bodies. So I fetched the hand-scrubber from the hut, and lay in the washing-trough, while he roughed the grainy scab off my back and front, and swilled me down. Then he went over me again, carefully, and pronounced me wholesome. After, I spent a while on him. The cold water stung and chilled us: and the stiff bristles brushed my thin skin into red here and there. We dressed numbly and went on fire-picket. The Sergeant made us clean out the fire-station. I was too broken even to look a protest.

We got back for roll-call, and bought ourselves a mess-tin of tea and three sausage rolls from the coffee-stall. At least I paid, having ninepence (Nobby and Sailor were wholly broke) while Sailor found the guts to go over and fetch it us. Boyne, being ex-officer, was over-nice for tuck. Then to bed but not, in my case, to sleep. Partly I was too tired: partly the smell of swill and refuse oozed slowly from my soiled things and stagnated into a pool over me. I lay staring into the black roof for hours, trying to forget the five days that must pass before my laundry went.

20

OUR COMMANDING OFFICER

I woke as the lights flashed on. A headache, a burning throat, a body which ached from head to foot as though a steam-roller had worked over me all night. Oh yes, of course, I was on shit-cart, yesterday. However, now it's P.T. and a new day.

Yet not good. The idiot gym-corporal, whose word of command Madden had likened to the sneeze of a cockroach, again took charge of us. Sergeant Cunninghame was on week-end and so this brute got master hand. To support him that lost soul, the Commandant, turned up. Many mornings he does, driving over in his two-seater. He is only the shards of a man —left leg gone, a damaged eye and brain (as we charitably suppose), one crippled arm, silver plates and corsets about his ribs. Once he was a distinguished soldier:—and now the R.A.F. is his pitying almoner.

For P.T. he does not wear his artificial limbs: instead he crutches himself with empty trouser-leg to the cook-house wall, and props himself against a buttress, while with his arm he attempts to follow the instructor's movements. Magnificent, you say, of a cripple so to defy his disability? Theatrical swank, done at our expense. He, being always resentfully in pain, is determined that we shall be at least uncomfortable. His presence drags out the P.T. to its uttermost minute: and however hard the sky may weep on us, the exercises must be gone through. Then he drives home to change his clothes, if in his ruins there is a bone whole enough to feel the chill of damp. The airmen have to walk these their only trousers dry.

The Corporal hustled us off our feet, barking and snarling. Everybody was sick of him, and the drill fell to pieces. The best instructor can make nothing of an unwilling squad: and this corporal was one of the worst. Cursing and threatening are barren means of instruction. On me the exhaustion of yesterday lay heavy, and the slippery asphalt made running more arduous. Once or twice I was nearly done; but they clouted me on as a slacker, and I staggered at it again. Eight fellows did actually fall out, instead of the usual daily two or three: but I have searched myself exhaustively, and know that I can hardly faint. As well, for if I did, the doctors might spin me as unfit, and then all these pains and hopes would have been wasted.

Of course I missed breakfast: for the strength of its food would have sickened my blown body. Afterwards Corporal Abner told me I was detailed as headquarters' runner for the day, and must get into blue at once and go over. It would be a chance for me to break in my 'horse-bandages':—the birds' nests in our puttees had mightily worried him before church parade. The R.A.F. issue puttee is inelastic, with no give to fit it round the leg like Fox's puttees, which are the first purchase of an airman with twelve shillings to spare: but at the Depot recruits may not go on parade in Fox's. So somehow these horse-bandages have to be made serviceable. Abner's tip was to put them on very tightly, wet: so they would stretch where strained, and shrink where loose, and after two or three such wettings would have fairly moulded themselves to the spring of our calf muscles. Meanwhile the torture of their compres-

85

sion crippled us. I was more a hobbler today than a runner: but still the messenger job promised to be clean and light, so I was grateful to the Corporal for choosing me.

At headquarters I was dumped on a form in the passage, till wanted: which was not for two hours. At intervals of about a minute officers came past. My orders were to rise to my feet each time in silent salutation. The plaster behind the runners' seat shone with the six-years' friction of their backs. It was a relief from the game of mechanised toy when the Sergeant Major had me set and light his fire.

Soon after eleven the Commandant sallied out to inspect the kit of a trained draft about to leave the Depot. Where he went I had to follow, like Mary's lamb, two paces behind him: and I was studying how to keep step with his dotting false leg when he swung round on me and shouted to know why the bloody hell I'd let the point of my stick droop towards the ground. The rage-distorted face was thrust down into mine, making me sick at the near squalor of those coarse hairs which bushed from his ears and nose, and the speckle of dark pits which tattooed his skin. 'What's your number?' (Incidentally, never call the fellows 'man'; and be careful to ask for their names first, not their number. We are not proud of being ticketed.) 'What's your squad?' 'I've not been squadded yet, Sir.' Beaten, he faced round and stumped on. Not even the arch-punisher could punish an undrilled man for a fault in drill. To inflict misery pleased him, for his body so pained him that only tight lips and a scowl kept him going: and it was an alleviation to see the circle of terror widen about him.

More shame was my portion in the hut, where the kit was exposed neatly on the beds. Without a glance, he thrust his stick under the blanket of the first lot, and flung it to the floor.

86 'Lay it out again, properly,' he thundered at the dazed owner.

The same with the second and third. By then he had assuaged his failure to put me in trouble and the other kits were not ravaged.

'That your best hat?' to one man. 'Yes, S-S-Sir,' he stammered. A knowing fellow. The Commandant liked men who cringed. He passed on. 'And yours?' to the next. 'Yes, Sir,' replied this one, undauntedly. The Commandant jerked the cap forward over the man's eyes, then pulled it off and threw it behind him. 'New cap,' he spat towards the sergeant at his elbow. 'New cap, Sir,' repeated the sergeant obsequiously. 'And put the man down for a regimental haircut,' he went on. That meant the clippers all over his head, and him a disfigured convict for weeks.

The bullying went further. I found myself trembling with clenched fists, repeating to myself, 'I must hit him, I must,' and the next moment trying not to cry for shame that an officer should so play the public cad. Fortunately this hut ended the performance, and we stalked back to headquarters in procession, Commandant, myself, Sergeant Major, Orderly Sergeant, Service Policeman. The fellows who saw our crocodile coming scuttled back or dodged behind huts. If the Commandant were on the road from the bridge we would go round to M. Section by the half-mile detour of the canteen, to rescue ourselves from the smart of his glance.

One day he started to walk across with a leashed dog in each hand. The excited beasts sprang forward after a cat. Down went the cripple, fairly pulled over on his face. He would not let go the dogs. Nor could he raise his blaspheming self. The slopes thickened with airmen silently watching him struggle. The contagion of interest reached the squads, and drill stopped. At last the duty officer, seeing the derelict, rushed down and set him again on foot. 'Let the old cunt rot,' had muttered airman to airman.

Yet were we kinder to him than his next command. The day he first flew there, the aerodrome was ringed with his men almost on their knees, praying he would crash. Such hate of a brave man is as rare as it is hurtful to the service. His character was compounded of the corruptions of courage, endurance, firmness and strength: he had no consideration for anyone not commissioned, no mercy (though all troops abundantly need mercy every day) and no fellowship. He leaned only to the military side of the Air Force, and had no inkling that its men were not amenable to such methods. Partly this may have been honest stupidity. His officer friends urged that he was kind to dogs, and had the men's material interests at heart. It was that which hurt us most. We felt that we should be more considered than our food and our clothes. He treated us like stock-cattle: so the sight of him became a degradation to us, and the overhearing his harsh tone an injury. His very neighbourhood grew hateful, and we shunned passing his house.

After dinner the Adjutant rang for me, and with manifold instructions handed over a sealed packet for the pay section across the bridge. That untidy hut seemed full of trestle tables loaded with documents, and I wandered about it unable, in the multitude of clerks, to find the one whose function it would be to relieve messengers of their responsibility. Dimly I became conscious of the gold braid marking an officer in the furthest recesses of the room. Suddenly he called, 'Don't you salute an officer?' In astonishment I gabbled out, 'Yes, Sir, if he has his hat on.' Stepping back a pace, he put a bewildered hand to his head and gasped, 'But I *have* mine on.' 'So you have, Sir,' replied I, gaily: and saluted him: and thrust my encumbering letter into his empty hands: and about-turned smartly into safe air before he could close his mouth.

The rest of the afternoon I was servant to the gentle-spoken

Adjutant, whose shy reluctance to use me fired me to forestall his orders. Four-thirty came, and the Commandant prepared to return home, my signal of release. I bore his attaché case and papers to the little car. He struggled hardly in, unhelped; for we knew that he would swipe at an offered hand with his crutch. On the seat he made room for the dog. I swung the engine. He waved me away while he let in the clutch and backed her round: then roared, 'Now jump, you damned fool!' I took a flying leap to the sloping back, and clung there apelike between the hood and the luggage rack while he drove smartly across the park to his tree-bowered house by the golf course.

He pulled up at its gate: and shouted to me, 'Attention!' I stood as if on parade. 'Carry your stick properly, next time. Fall out!' I turned to the right, saluted and marched off. Only by having companions in misfortune is the absurdity of being drilled made bearable. So my back, as I walked away, was blushing with the idea that my legs were not stepping straightly, to his eyes. They were sore legs, too. My shrinking puttees were a good reason for my wish that he had not inflicted on me this long walk back to the camp. Before I was out of earshot I could hear him loudly drilling his little children, in the garden.

21

THE SOCIAL CODE

Sergeant Lawton, who has general supervision of the fatigue parties, gave me to the camp barber, for today. This job sometimes lets us wangle a free haircut, if trade's slack. Otherwise there is not much in it: the fatigue man keeps the stove burning, sweeps the floors every hour or so and, when there are many customers, lathers in readiness the chins of those awaiting shaves.

A quiet job: but out of it I got a social shock, when the barber began our hut chant of 'Sally.' Did the fellow think himself a man, like us? Troops are so cabined in their private world that they believe the services hold a monopoly of manliness. In them, all we are bound and equal: except this one is quicker-limbed at drill, or that one more experienced. Of class-difference there isn't a suspicion. In our hut newspaper boys and Cambridge undergrads lived level, and tried to speak the same choppy airmen-dialect. But civvies, like this barber, aren't in the picture. His familiar friendliness disagreeably stiffened me. Odd.

Tonight China came back in a mess. He had got half-drunk in the town, and had taken a tart down the canal towpath, to shag her. There he quarrelled with two bargemen: probably his fault, for he is impossibly foul-mouthed, when canned. One he hit: the other blacked his eye. He fell, got a kick in the belly, and rolled into shallow water. When he staggered through the hut to his bed, he was silent and white-faced: but he was always white, with a face of sourness and lewdness incomparable. All thought him merely fuddled. He undressed to the skin, which confirmed our guess. The poorer the man, the more shy of nakedness. We much miscall the officers for their public-school fashion of loosely walking their bedrooms, undressed, before batmen.

He sprawled over the bed, rolling his head queerly and bowing his trunk backward over the head-rail and pillow, with gasps which turned to groans. Then we gathered round, and in a stifled string of oaths he explained his scrap with two civvies who hadn't fought fair. His eyes closed, and his ribs pumped in and out with a struggle for breath. He seemed bad. Feebly he piped for Sailor, his pal.

Sailor came with a leap over the central stall of the hut: and when he had heard the cause of trouble, began to massage his abdomen, heartily. After ten minutes China was lying at peace on the bed. Snaggletooth went to the coffee-bar (which a humane custom permitted till midnight just inside the gate, to refresh those coming in off late pass) and brought back a mess-tin of hot tea. China drank, and slowly fell asleep. In the morning he was at P.T. just as usual, the performance of the night before clean out of memory. I think it had been a craving for sympathy after his beating. Besides, Boyne, our precise ex-officer, had been with China and witnessed the fight: avoiding it, because China was in the wrong. This was a sin against the code of Clerkenwell and Boyne was less of our company, after.

Public-school and state-school do not mix easily. In a pillow-fight some evenings ago several bolster-cases were torn. The Corporal asked for the names of the guilty. Everyone stood

91

mum. Corporal Abner waited a confession: none came. So he pronounced sentence upon us all. We should do three successive fire-pickets, and the damage be stopped in a levy on our pay. An hour later Horder (ex-Haileybury), leader of the pillow-fight, returned off fatigue. When he heard the news he went up to Corporal Abner and declared himself the prime cause and responsible. So we got off free: but the hut was puzzled and resentful. 'Prick, to go bobbing round the Corp and taking things on hisself. Fuck the fire-picket.' He had nipped our pleasure in combining to lie low and take a hut-punishment. We begin to want to be a squad, not individuals.

22

BREAKING OR MAKING

The little chief-instructor again took us for P.T., quietly and kindly, despite the Commandant's malevolent eye upon his back. His orders came as though he liked us; and gently, as a man talking. We had to behave ourselves to hear him. Whilst he was making us jump and flap our arms at once, one clumsy fellow failed to synchronise the rhythm and sequence of his limbs—arms came down while legs went up, or both waved wildly together, as though he was trying to 'take off.' A laugh started at the sight. Sergeant Cunninghame marched out to the front (yet in all good-humour) those who laughed, not the failure. Every other instructor would have laughed at me with the majority. Did the grim Commandant, propped away against his wall, learn anything?

Our fatigue today was in the gymnasium. They were making a sports ground and our job was to wire-brush and repaint a lot of salvaged sheeting with which to fence the running track. A good job, it looked. Six of us and six wire brushes: but these were mangy things, with half their bristles missing and half broken-short. Whilst the corporal sent for new ones we watched the squads on the bars, or boxing, or vaulting the horse. Our athletes rejoiced at the plays of muscle awaiting us. Alas, how cheerfully would I for ever forgo all play!

There were no other brushes. We must carry on slabbing the paint over the rust and scale. The useless labour demoralised us into unwilling frauds: and went to confirm the suspicion that they were desperately finding pretexts to keep us busy. We bitterly feel that in this dragged month has been spilled the zeal of our new-coming, which might have carried us over the drudgery of drill and square, into service. An ill-directed zeal, of course. Our raw hands in their eagerness try to clean both inside and out: and therefore fail in speed and are cursed for laziness. But old soldiers, who never waste a minute or a hand's turn on the parts that do not show, achieve both praise and economy of means.

So far we get only the curses, defencelessly. Here in Depot are four hundred recruits, sixty officers, a hundred sergeants and corporals. So every third man has the power to change our courses. Most of them do. We are tossed through the day, haphazardly, from hand to hand like the golden balls of a juggler: and with some of the apprehension of the balls, lest we be dropped suddenly and bruised. Bruised, not broken: and that makes part of the sorrow. We can be half-killed, not killed: punished but not capitally. There is no thrill of a real danger to graze and avoid: only the certainty of minor accident, and no way of escape—from a self-built prison? How can we? It induces an expedient truckling: for it is lighter to bear injustice than to explain.

I think the sudden barking of sergeants and sergeant majors on parade always denotes a miscarriage of authority, wanting to spread blind terror. They have transformed us fifty civilians into very frightened troops in a few days. Our squadron leader put it well at office to two of us who were 'up' for having dirty boots on fire-picket, the evening of their turn at shit-cart. He said, 'I do not want to have your excuses. You are not here on

94

trial, nor am I judging you. My duty is to support the authority of the sergeant who has thought fit to run you before me. Three days to barracks.' If only they were all so honest. It is the pretence (or broken hope) of justice which hurts.

We recruits are counselled always the road of least resistance, to dodge everything earned or unearned—except our pay. At the end of every such exhortation we remind one another, 'Let's remember we are soldiers': to be corrected by yells of 'Airmen,' or if the Corporal's gone 'Royal Airmen,' in derision. Day and night the distinction between airmen and soldiers is dinned into us by all comers: and we learn it the more willingly for that it consoles us against our pains of fatigue or drill to think that there exist fellows for whom these military futilities are a welcome profession.

We identify the army with its manner of life and already sincerely despise and detest it. 'Fuck the military,' cat-calls China. 'All prick and no money.' Soldiers are parts of a machine and their virtue is in subordinating themselves within their great company. Airmen are lords and masters, when not slaves, of their machines, which the officers indeed own in the air but which belong to us individually for the longer hours they are on earth. Not here of course in the Depot. Here we cannot get away from the degrading drill which in our after-life as serving airmen will be only punitive, a part of jankers.

It is perhaps a pity they have no sign in the Depot of the R.A.F.'s proper business—no sign other than the Bristol Fighter moulting behind bars in the Transport Yard. The sight of flying would hearten us, as a reminder of our profession—to help conquer the air. We are vowed to this enterprise (a corporate effort in which no more names can be pre-eminent: but success will visit the joined hands of a million obscure) to win the freehold of the upper element in as full measure as man's licence on land, or a sailor's liberty at sea. After which I should note that only one other in the hut has wished aloud to go up in the air. Several have hoped they will not have the chance.

Yet, whether keen to fly or not, we are airmen, with the new character the new force is making for itself. About the R.A.F. there is nothing military except the intelligence of some of its officers. Airmen go scatty when the public call them 'Privates in the Air Force.' Deliberately, punctiliously, to the point of folly, the Air Ministry has made its service unlike either Army or Navy. Look at our ranks! Aircraftmen second-class (all of us now), ditto first-class, leading aircraftmen. Unwieldy stupidities of names! Ourselves we shorten them to LAC, AC I, AC II, and speak of ourselves as 'ack-emmas' (the air mechanic of the Great War) or 'urks.'[1] Urk corresponds with matlow or swaddy, the fellows' own name for their serving condition.

[1] In the last line but two, 'irk' is corrected to 'urk,' but in later passages there is no change made.

23

COOK'S MATE

Again unlucky. I've been picked for kitchen fatigue which we know by experience to be the worst, after shit-cart, of our drudgeries. No P.T. anyway. Kitcheners crawl out of bed into overalls and go straight over at the dark reveille, unwashed, to work till the guard have had their suppers after seven at night. These are long hours, and the tepid dishwater: the smooth evil of grease: the having to hump great quarters of chilled beef, smelling like corpses, from meat lorry to cutting bench: the inevitable sodding of hands, and hair and clothes with a reek which will cling in them for days: all these are particular miseries to anyone who hates kitchens and the apparatus of flesh-food. In a bakery, now, there is not such foulness.

As extra, wanton misery today for me was a young cook whose voice in the clangorous kitchen could very well take off the yap of a puppy. He was proud of this mastery and had studied to find from which corner it was loudest. Already the place was discordant as a boiler factory and his 'Wow Wow Wow Yap' every few minutes seemed to craze my brain, like someone stitching it through and through with steel needles. If, as I think, I most fear animal spirits in this world, so do

I most hate noise, which jangles me till I thrum like a tautened string.

My body has been unpleasantly taut since I enlisted and silly accidents have further extended me. A fortnight ago I broke a little finger stumbling on the wet tarmac at P.T. and last Friday I sprained my instep carrying a double sack of flour down the steps to M. cook-house. The dim lights of the hut make first my eyes ache, and then my head, while I pencil these notes. So the whole state of man is presently miserable. I feel my unfitness, not for the Air Force life which I have tasted and found good, but for the severities of this recruits' course. Also I am failing to write down its power, as signally as I fail to live it. The thing is alluringly big: but how put back the clock of my body so that I may have carelessness to see it? How spin words when I am afraid for myself all day?

The weakness of will and body, which let the barking cook distress me into shiverings, also put me across the disfavour of the tubby chief-cook, a dung-beetle in shape and manner—but a crimson dung-beetle—who busily conveyed and caught and hid from the orderly officer his pickings of our food. It sickened me to be made part of a superior's felonies: and as I stole for him, so I let what I thought show in my eyes. It was hard to keep it only to my eyes. Once again my fists were crisping. For relief I worked hotly, scouring his beastly coppers and pans till they shone with an excess of surface: and that was a new offence. He wanted them only to pass the casual scrutiny of daily inspection. He knew my painstaking was a defiant judgment upon himself. 'You're good at bull-shit,' he wheezed, knowing that word of praise would insult any airman: 'now come and set out my knives and forks.' This was reprisal: he wasted two hours of my day sizing and dressing in futile ranks the cutlery they were about to use. Yet I'm glad the fat hash-slinger was peeved into reaction.

We served dinner to the queued-up orderlies. My puppy-cook charged himself with dishing out the custard, whose yellow suavity was to ease the sharpness of boiled apple. He leaped thighs-astride the warm copper that held it; riding up and down with 'Ah, Ah, Ah' and heaving loins, in pretence it was a woman. Intermittently he licked round the ladle's rim with his slobby tongue. Because we did not laugh, he cocked an eye at us and declared loudly, 'There are three sorts of turd:—mustard,' with a whack at the aluminum cruet on the table:—'custard,' flinging a splodge of it upon Madden, who stood by me:—'and your bloody little self.'

When, very late in the evening, I opened the door of our shining hut there met me such noise as if a lodge of demons were revelling within. Sailor took me under the armpits and jazzed me past the basin and comb band to the far door and back. 'We're for inspection tomorrow by Squadron-Leader: that means squadding. Thank Christ, O thank Christ.' Behind me Peters, the sarcastic, came in from London. 'You're all very happy,' he sneered. 'Go and fuck rattlesnakes,' retorted Garner, 'I'm always happy when I'm broke and have clicked a fire-picket.' Then we told him the truth, but he would not believe it. 'You're pulling my pisser: our mob's on fatigue for the duration.'

Something of the sort we had begun to whisper, as week followed week without respite. Had the Air Force forgotten its promise when we enlisted, in its need of a maintenance party for the Depot? After the sixth week there had been acid protests in the hut: suggestions we should do this or that to assert ourselves. Rebellious again? Not on your life. I think it is hundreds of years since the Commons of England had a grievance that did not purge with grumbling. But now we had our wish, and the prospect of square was relatively golden. We had seen enough of it from our distance to dread it wholesomely. No recruit left Depot without a hatred of drill to last him his seven years. But square had an end: fatigues never. Squadding means escape, one day.

24

INSPECTION

It's the first time our crowd's seen an officer close to, except when receiving punishment. No, there was the doctor who vaccinated and inoculated us with immense care, that first Tuesday. Strange he should have kept interest in the technicalities of a job he must do one hundred times a week. Even his eyes seemed to see each one of us, apart, before he stabbed us. Otherwise the practice of the Depot was to set an irrefragable bar of non-commissioned officers between us and our natural leaders. It gave the place a foreign tone, like the Prussian Army or the Legion: and orphaned us yet further. N.C.O.s were graduated, from the magnificently self-esteemed first Sergeant Major (tall, splay-footed, voiced like a costive crow) to the jealous touchiness of corporals. Corporals were of all kinds; but the importance of sergeants! The set lips, the momentous tread, the Roman poise of the hat (all hat and no head, often), the ox-weight and dignity. The back of a sergeant's neck is brick-red, thick and hairless. They have slow eyes. Their natures have put away all childish things.

We stood in sized ranks before the Orderly Room. Stiffy, the Drill Adjutant, who is the beginning and the end of training in the Depot, walked with fierce fixed stare down our line. He puffed out his chest, as if saying, 'Will any of you worms

101

dare to face me, pretending a right to live?' Before each man with ribbons on tunic he halted to ask details of previous service. If he confessed Navy, the military moustache perceptibly twitched. Stiffy was Guards—a sergeant-instructor—and don't forget it! Better forget his commission in the R.A.F. It is the Guards' esprit de corps which makes the normal soldier hate them enviously. We can't believe in anything as they believe in their mob.

Finally Stiffy ordered, 'Ex-service to the right: first enlistments left.' I shuffled left amongst the younger fellows. It will be gayer to see the inexperienced making their own vices. We are 5 Squad and the old soldiers 4 Squad. I was regretting the loss of Sailor, when I saw him and Lofty, the lank Marconibloke, and Cook returning to the fold. Stiffy wouldn't pass the Navy as part-trained. 'Calls yer a bloody rookie, does 'e?' scoffed the glad China. 'Old soldier old cunt,' retorted Sailor. Corporal Abner hissed Silence at us. Kit inspection in fifteen minutes. We broke into a mad rush.

In rehearsal, kit-laying had taken an hour. First we rolled down our mattresses, and covered them with our brownest and least-torn blanket. The other bedding made a chocolate sandwich at the bed-head. On it we laid our great-coats, pressed as square as a box, with polished buttons winking down the front. On top of that our blue caps. We stood back in the alleyway, and trued the pile upright.

Now the tunic, so folded that the belt made it a straight edge. Covering it, the breeches, squared to the exact area of the tunic, with four concertina-folds facing forward. Towels were doubled once, twice, thrice, and flanked the blue tower. In front of the blue sat a rectangular cardigan. To each side a rolled puttee. Shirts were packed and laid in pairs like flannel bricks. Before them, pants. Between them, neat balls of socks, wedged in. Our holdalls were stretched wide, with knife, fork, spoon, razor, comb, toothbrush, lather brush, button-stick, in that order, ranged across them. Into the displayed house-wives were stuck needles ready threaded with khaki cotton. Our spare boots were turned soles-up, each side of the holdall. The soles had been polished black and the steel tips and five rows of hobnails rubbed with emery-paper, to shine. Our five polishing brushes, washed and with glass-papered white backs, were lined across the foot of the bed.

All our official effects were so on view, mathematically spaced, folded, measured and weighed: also largely numbered with our official numbers. That gave the game away. Airmen, for dislike of being ticketed, will not wear garments which are visibly numbered. This stuff was just kit-inspection stuff, and our real dirty brushes, our really worn clothes were hidden in our boxes. 'Proper bull-shit,' grumbled Lofty when made to Silvo his boot-blacking tin till it simulated silver. Bull-shit it was.

The Squadron Leader, ex-Navy himself, blew freshly round the hut, not looking at the careful kits, but speaking to each man. A recollection of the savage Commandant made me thankful not all R.A.F. officers disgraced their rank. His eyes lit on my books, and he bent down to my locker—scrubbed spotless inside and out—to read their backs. 'What's that?' he asked of Niels Lyhne. 'Oh, you read Danish: why did you join the Air Force?' 'I think I had a mental break-down, Sir.' 'What, what? What! Sergeant Major, take his name.' He passed on. 'Office nine o'clock,' said the Sergeant Major curtly, with a gleam in his eye.

I was marched in under escort. The Flight Lieutenant was grave. He could give me only seven days and the crime of insolence to a Senior Officer demanded extreme rigour. At

103

last he remanded me for trial by the Squadron Leader I had apparently insulted. 'A good game this: shot at dawn, probably,' I said to myself not really caring a tinker's curse. We had all been on defaulters', the R.A.F. punishment, already. 'Jankers,' our affectionate name for it, is mainly an irritant, especially at Depot, for recruits' crimes were expunged from their sheets, when they passed out. There is an hour's drill, in equipment and full pack. That is a mild strain, which leaves the muscles aching. Afterwards come extra fatigues, a joke to us, who already do all a man can do. In the intervals we must visit the guard-room every hour, to report. A man regrets his first dose, bitterly, for it is the loss of his clean sheet: and every recruit begins with the fantastic aim of completing his seven years without a crime. Fantastic, because many senior N.C.O.s chase their subjects till they have got them a dose each. After that, it's a swank to collect many entries. All in our hut were case-hardened—so far as 'Office' was concerned —in less than six weeks.

At last I was run in, guarded and bareheaded, for trial by my cause of offence. When the charge was repeated he burst into laughter. 'Bless my Sowl, Sergeant Major; bless my howly Sowl. I told you to take his name in case we wanted an intelligent man for a job. What damned fool drafted this charge? Get out!' He swiped me, friendly, across the backside with his stick. They say I'm the first man to dodge a charge laid by our S.M. Perhaps. I'm bobbing on not getting that intelligent job from him! In the afternoon we moved to Hut 4.

25

HUMBUGGING ABOUT

Yesterday, it was, that we moved huts, from Two into Four. Last night, as the survivors of Two sat together, there hung over us a sense of regret, of loss, of being lost. We had been so obedient to Corporal Abner that we had forgotten the habit of decision. No other corporal has been assigned us, and we feel neglected at not being overseen. It will be curious if service experience takes altogether away our power of free navigation. Very curious in my case, after the wilful life in which I seemed so set. Now my will has apparently turned against self: despite outside discouragement. The trouble I had to get into the Air Force at all! Surely for less work I could have had my seat in the Cabinet!

In the morning when we woke up it was as if we had never been in any other place. Yet the need of a master cried aloud in us: so we fell ourselves properly in, under Sailor, to manage P.T. and breakfast in the way of uniformity. We are now hardened to P.T. and avoid its acerbities. The younger irks can laugh and play among the half-made beds, when they come off it: but I am distressed till the afternoon. Of course it is partly mental, this distress. I have wished myself to know that any deliberate exercise or display of the body is a prostitution; our created shapes being only our accidents until by taking pleasure or pains in them we make them our fault. Therefore the having to be attentive to my arms and legs is the bitterest part of the bill I pay for this privilege of enlistment.

My determined endeavour is to scrape through with it, into the well-paid peace of my trade as photographer to some squadron. To that I look forward as profession and livelihood for many years:—for good, I hope, since the stresses of my past existence give me warrant, surely, for thinking that my course will not be too long. How welcome is death, someone said, to them that have nothing to do but to die.[1]

Meanwhile there is this training to be gone through, desperately, with my refuge at stake. Half a dozen times I have nearly cracked: but not very lately. Every week things seem easier. I can eat the food now—provided I miss a meal a day: it's a prize-fighter diet they give us. If only I could sleep solidly! but desert experience taught me to hover through the nights in a transparent doze, listening for the threat of any least sound or movement: and in a hut of fifty strong fellows there is not one minute of night-silence.

We worked today on the new sports' stadium. Carpenters had put a three-barred pale round it, and our job was to spike this over with corrugated iron sheets, to shut the running track off from camp view. The work was heavy for a party of three, but when done was at least something tangible. Five years later I was warmed by the sight of it yet standing firm. Also on such a day as this it was good to be in the open air.

Our taskmaster was a little corporal, who had just slipped out of a charge of theft. He had been bringing back the body of a recruit from the railway line behind the camp: and something which had been in the dead lad's pocket was found in the wrong place. However the evidence was not sufficient:

106   [1] Alas: in March 1935 my engagement ran out. J.H.R.

though we, who had known poor Benson before he killed himself (young fellows, shyly bred, were too often overwhelmed when they tried to breast the whole wave of life at once), knew, perhaps, more than the officers wished to know.

Corporal Hardy lay on his back in the grass behind the fence, and lazed in the sun's warmth, watching through his narrowed eyelids how we worked. We gave him warning if anyone serious loomed up. Whenever one of the metal sheets slipped from the fingers of the holding man, we wished for the Corporal's help: but nothing doing. This, he said, was his holiday: before he took charge of our hut. Well, he has been nearly scalded; so perhaps he will be easy.

We worked for days on this fence. The Second Sergeant Major said we seemed to have the hang of it and might continue. It felt always like fine weather, and the scent of deep, brown grass, and the feel of sun-warmed iron are not my least memories of the Depot. We were now careless of the delay. It had a term. We were squadded men, just waiting for their instructor to come back off leave, and we might as well do this as nothing, or something worse. The knowing beforehand what was our work on the morrow made the lying down at night and the rising up at dawn assured and pleasing.

26

CHINA'S TROUBLE

Last night, taking advantage of there being no corporal in the hut, China, our lurid Cockney, crossed after lights out to Snaggletooth's bed and had a half-hour's whispering with him. Snaggle (one of his incisors had been snapped across the middle) is a man of twenty-four, reliant and knowledgeable, who did six years in the Army; though he wouldn't admit it to Stiffy the other day. I guessed China was in trouble, and saw its traces at fatigue-time next day, when he was silent and more than ordinarily bitter-faced. Not that the look of this pallid whirlwind-biting sneerer was ever a whit genial.

The afternoon was Saturday and our off time. I had a craving to lose sight, for a moment, of this camp which has been part bagnio, part ergastulum, and, till of late, wholly disagreeable. So I dressed all in my shoddy glory, and walked towards the little town. By the tram-stop outside the Seven Bells stood China, biting his nails on the kerb, a picture of uncertain discontent. When two airmen cross on a pavement they exchange an esoteric wink: but China put out his hand, 'Half a minute, Bo.' He walked into the road, gazed down the empty tramline, came back and said hoarsely, urgently: 'Come and have a drink.' I hesitated: China's drinking would be death and damnation to me: but clearly such urgency had cause. I went inside.

'Mine's a bitter,' he confided in his half-whisper. 'Yours a small port?' His notion of a posh drink: and in the hut I'm posh, not for my bookish accent (pound-note talk) but for having the only active wrist-watch. Not ten times but fifty times a day I have to call out the hour, by request. Being patient, always I do it exactly: and in return courtesy they defer to me, when they seek something, as 'Mister.'

However, the drinks were served. A crony of China's, corporal of service police, was drawn into our round. China began to jerk out that his bird had turned up from Londonderry, that day, to find him; and now he must straightway marry her. He'd met her when he was garrison in Ireland, and had told her that as soon demobbed he'd join the R.A.F. So she had searched him out. 'Must you marry her?' asked the Corporal. 'Well, a girl with guts enough to come across and find me . . . she's a boxer; a proper champ.' China was so moved that he forgot his f. and b. adjectives. The Corporal agreed one must play up to a girl like that. A champion boxer: just so. The next round was on me.

China was yet ill at ease: bleak: miserable. There was more. It seemed he had been warned yesterday that on Tuesday he was to leave for Halton where he'd been posted for training. Short notice: but the Corporal knew Halton; and encouraged him. She could enter the R.A.F. hospital there, and get it over. A bramah hospital. . . . China interrupted, trembling, 'Yes, that's three bastard fucking days off. Where the fucking hell am I to get the girl lodgings in this cunting place? The old girl gave her three quid for coming over. They're R.C. like me. It'll have to be a civvy marriage: can't square the padre by Monday.' He was near crying. The Corporal began an air-force-law explanation of what China must do. 'The Old Man's married' (that's the Squadron Leader for whom I suffered last

109

week); 'he won't be hard on you, if you tell him all about it. He'll let you off light.'

The tram was heard, and the Corporal left us to air his police armlet on the pavement. He had spoken decently, to my surprise. The army has a rule that N.C.O.s mayn't consort with privates—or rather, there was such a rule before the war. In the R.A.F. all men are equal: an amendment which makes much for efficiency and modesty. But we don't count service police as men. Unhappy hybrids:—they can earn their fellows' praise only as they neglect their duty.

China gloomily offered another drink. A pity the Corporal's duty had abstracted him when it was his turn. I was scenting lack of money as China's trouble, so took the round myself, being careful to let him see the two pounds in my pocket. 'If the cash would be of any use, China?' . . . He grabbed at it like a drowner. 'Christ Almighty: hope you'll not want to be paid right now. . . . Well, I'm buggered, who'd have fucking well thought it.' Leaving the drink he rushed out and on to the east-bound tram, after wringing my hand to the bone: I took my penniless way back to camp. The money was what he'd wanted all the time, but his hardness had made him too brittle to ask me directly. Also he'd needed the relief of confession to his unlikeliest confidant. We'd lived together since August: yet, only two days ago, he'd told little Nobby I was a deep fucker, whom he couldn't sort of size up.

You see, I cannot play at anything with anyone: and a native shyness shuts me out from their freemasonry of fucking and blinding, pinching, borrowing, and talking dirty: this despite my sympathy for the abandon of functional frankness in which they wallow. Inevitably, in our crowded lodging, we must communicate just those physical modesties which polite life keeps veiled. Sexual activity's a naïve boast, and any abnormalities of appetite or organ are curiously displayed. The Powers encourage this behaviour. All latrines in camp have lost their doors. 'Make the little buggers sleep and shit and eat together,' grinned old Jock Mackay, senior instructor, 'and we'll have 'em drilling together, naturally.' But China and I had defeated him. In camp we were strangers: and the wall of our strangeness broke down only here, outside camp bounds, when he and I were the two surviving spots of blue in a world of plain clothes.

27

A SERMON

Our holiday continues. Still there is no corporal in the hut. So we planned a lie-in this Sunday morning, getting up just nicely for breakfast in the warm comfort of daylight. Use, however, roused us at the habitual six o'clock. We lay curled in our beds and chatted. A large leisured opening of the day. There was a dissolute raffishness in thus taking ease under the long nose of authority. Lofty, our six-foot-two weed of a naval telegraphist, unfolded himself from the bed, and in his short shirt (the same size shirt as that which tightly filled the trouser-butt of little me) paraded with his sheet before each of us, triumphantly showing its traces of wet dreams. 'This top one,' he boasted, 'is the dead spit of a map of Ireland.' Sailor was curt with him. 'You should leave off pulling your plonk.' Lofty, the grinning, chicken-hearted fool, protested with a break of feeble indignation in his throat. 'I'm engaged to the best bride in Devonport, and it's of her I dream every night. Since we fixed it up I haven't tasted cunt. A bloke knows when he's well off.'

A fine morning for church parade. The whole R.A.F. band had turned out, and during our division into flights, and sizing, and arrangement, they made plaintively beautiful music of the Christchurch call, by the sheer slow richness of their reeds.

These became our sentiments, too. Worship seemed due from us on so sunny a morning: though I missed my posh space by the font, and had no mediaeval art to entertain me. Only the tombstone (without virtues) of Mr. Daniel Stonard who died in 1724, aged nineteen. I'm glad I've lived this long, anyway.

So perforce I heard another unreal service, and again its misapplication stung me, preached as it was over the serried ranks of those healthy irks I knew from the skins upward. Now they were alike-dressed, and all singing 'The King of Love My Shepherd Is' with the voices and the pagan enjoyment of their everyday blaspheming. Nor did their minds see any contradiction between their worship and their life. Neither their clean words nor their dirty words had a significance. Words were like our boots, dirty on the fields, clean indoors: a daily convention, no index of the fellows' mind. They had not learned to speak.

The blind padre was still labouring to draw a response from the dumb. The truckling humility of his general confession, his tremendous pretence of absolution, jarred across the blue congregation—as stridently as would one of our oaths across a hushed church. Simply there was no contact between these worlds. The fellows were mask-less, transparently unhesitant to declare their inmost or their whole purpose, practising the sinless honesty of all things clearly done. Such openness was holy.

Nor did we afford the padre justification for his opposing Man and God. By looking too inwardly upon his single self, such a one could see his spirit divorced from mankind and Godkind at once, and so stand physically preaching his trichotomy from the pulpit; while mentally he, somewhere in loneliness, considered the animals how they lived. But hardly in a

113

service. Enlistment brought the shock of a rediscovery of the basis of life:—in the troops' phrase, that every jack-man had his bicycle pump and tool-bag. In our boldest thrustings across the furthest airs, we carry that equipment with us: and uniformed men mean too much to each other to leave room for paracletes. Each of us is a little part of all the rest—as all the rest of us.

The parade ended without a formality of goose-stepping round the square. Nor did any shattered death's head glower upon us from beside the flag. I lay in the grass all afternoon, with the sunlight melting the week's aches out of me, joint by joint, till my whole being glowed with welfare.

28

OUR MOULD OF FORM

Such weather I may still enjoy, but slowly the park is fading from my mind. Partly it may be because the nights are not so warm that I can pleasantly pace the way by the river: partly because my feet are too tired at the end of the day any more to bear musing up and down. So I squat on my bed in the hut answering the fellows if they speak to me or trying to sleep early: for my broken nights give me a craving for longer oblivion. But mostly the park fades because the square is taking strong possession of our minds:—that square of tarmac on which the Air Force is going to re-shape our clay. A sharp ordeal. We study and pity the others enduring it.

Just for twelve weeks, we say: and beyond is the warm thought of our sheltering trades, after we are posted to some ordinary station: a return to the natures that were ours before enlistment. Yet we deceive ourselves, so colouring the future: for the lessons here are biting deep, and we shall never be the old selves again. Does it not rather frighten the R.A.F. to re-make so many men after its desire?

Bodily we are being built to drill-book pattern: spiritually we are being moulded nearly as fast. We are very unlike the loose civvies who drifted through the gate before Sergeant Sheepshanks two months back. The boastful ones have sunk down out of hearing, and the slow ones are haggard with being chased and chewed up (to arse-paper, as we say) by authority's angry mouth. Our sincerities save us not at all from humiliation and punishment. Therefore the high-spirited mope often; and break out against the sealed pattern, sometimes.

This Royal Air Force is not antique and leisurely and storied like an army. We can feel the impulsion of a sure, urging giant behind the scurrying instructors. Squad 5 is today the junior unit of the service. There are twenty thousand airmen better than us between it and Trenchard, the pinnacle and our exemplar: but the awe of him surely encompasses us. The driving energy is his, and he drives furiously. We are content, imagining that he knows his road. The Jew said that God made man after his own image—an improbable ambition in a creator. Trenchard has designed the image he thinks most fitted to be an airman; and we submit our nature to his will, trustingly. If Trenchard's name be spoken aloud in the hut, every eye swivels round upon the speaker, and there is a stillness, till someone says, 'Well, what of Trenchard?' and forthwith he must provide something grandiose to fit the legend. 'I reckon he's a man's man,' said James, in laughing admiration, one day, after several fellows had been swapping yarns of Trenchard's short way with Commanding Officers, our superb tyrants. China, the iconoclast, revolted. 'And I reckon,' he said, 'that Trenchard's shit smells much the same as mine.' The others cried him down.

The word Trenchard spells out confidence in the R.A.F. and we would not lose it by hearing him decried. We think of him as immense, not by what he says, for he is as near as can be inarticulate:—his words barely enough to make men think they divine his drift:—and not by what he writes, for he makes the least use of what must be the world's worst handwriting:—but

116

just by what he is. He knows; and by virtue of this pole-star of knowledge he steers through all the ingenuity and cleverness and hesitations of the little men who help or hinder him.

Trenchard invented the touchstone by which the Air Council try all their works. 'Will this, or will this not, promote the conquest of the air?' We wish, sometimes, the Air Council would temper wisdom to their innocent sheep. For instance, they have just decreed that the black parts of bayonets be henceforward burnished. That gives each man about twenty hours' work a year. Twenty hours is two-and-a-half days for we work eight hours on average and find time, by hook or crook, in official hours for all such Air Council luxuries. Rack their brains as they will, the irks cannot connect polished bayonets with flying efficiency. The fault is on us. Yet how can this brightness dangling at our left hips as we go to church be worth half a week, five thousand pounds a year, to Trenchard? If it were Stiffy now! The Guards polish their bayonets. But what a mess the Guards 'd make of our job.

117

29

THE LAST FATIGUE

Today we were chosen to bring in Decauville material from a derelict aerodrome six miles to the southward. Twelve of our squad, in two lorries: with a colourless sergeant-in-charge, and a physically vigorous corporal, who lent us all day his two ham-hands, and the thrust of his bulging hips, whenever there was a heavy lift. Seldom have I seen a man whose legs more fully required the width of a pair of trousers: and they were wide trousers. Yet he might have been poured into them, to set solid.

We were gay: yesterday Sergeant Jenkins, our Instructor-to-be, had returned off leave. So our probation was finished. There were lots of new recruits to take over our job of doing the Depot's chores: for the Air Ministry broke the hearts of its successive generations of recruits with this purgatory of fatigues, only to save the wages of fifty men on permanent camp maintenance. However, our successors would have to weep their own tears. 'Hope the poor buggers go through it, same as us,' said James, charitably. Tomorrow we should be on square.

The out journey in the empty lorries had therefore to be a jest: and we gave all-comers the chance to share our jest.

'Beaver!' we yelled at every bearded man (it was the period

118

of the Sitwells' silly game), and every girl was waved to, by our boiler-suited crew. As the lorry ground on its way through the villages we gallantly raised the age for girls, till every presentable woman received notice.

School-children cheered us over their playground walls: our five men with the racing engine made a fair return. Policemen we hooted. For old men the slogan was 'Mouldy.' We were all young, you see. We passed two trim airmen on the road, with shrieks of 'Up yer' and the Air greeting, of the right arm outflung, while the extended first and second fingers are jerked sharply upward. 'Shit in it,' they called back, rudely. We mewed like cats at an old woman.

And me? I had shrunk into a ball and squatted, hands over face, crying babily (the first time for years) on one corner of the scudding lorry, which rattled like a running skeleton, and at each leap dinted the impression of one projecting bolt or other into my substance. I was trying to think, if I was happy, why I was happy, and what was this overwhelming sense upon me of having got home, at last, after an interminable journey . . . word-dandling and looking inward, instead of swaying upright in the lorry with my pals, and yelling Rah Rah at all we met, in excess of life. With my fellows, yes; and *among* my fellows: but a fellow myself? Only when in concert we obeyed some physical movement, whose pattern could momently absorb my mind.

Just then we passed the canal, where barge-families sat sunning themselves on cabin-roofs. Enthusiasm burst all bounds, and provoked its bargee response. Our mild Sergeant in the leading lorry stopped and adjured us, as a crowd of hooligans, for the love of Mike to stop our sodding row. Half a mile on we screamed: 'Stop, stop!' agony and terror in our tones. The driver, a man of action, pulled up in a thirty-yard skid. 'What for fuck's sake's the matter now?' protested the angry Sergeant, to an empty lorry. Everyone was back up the road, cleaning out a chance-met coffee-stall. Then our driver, canny Yorkshireman, grew confused over the way, and halted to enquire it, under the laden branches of an orchard. The apples slaked our throats, finely.

By afternoon some of the spirit had evaporated from the party. Yet altogether we ran eight lorry loads of the Decauville rails for levelling the Depot's new hockey pitch, and six loads of hand-trucks on a Foden steamer. We picknicked for dinner off bread and bully and apples in the old aerodrome. Our hands were raw with blood-blisters. Our last fatigue: and good value to Trenchard.

PART TWO

In the Mill

Nearly three days pass

1

DISCIPLINES

Wednesday, October the fourth: only our third evening as a Flight, only three days completed on the square; yet from what seems a grey distance blurring by its lapse all first impressions, at last I attempt a note on our new life. The night is younger than used to be my writing-time: it's before nine o'clock, indeed. Then, at this hour, only two or three beds would have carried figures: but tonight, and last night, and the night before, each bed's been loaded with its prone man: and the hut is blanketed with fatigue.

Our first day was a dizzying whirl: our second the bleared fog of exhaustion: and the third? today? Well, for myself traces of light appear about the issue of our trial: but the rest are prostrate. In these days I have been a little better than them. My purgatory was passed during the fatigue period, and surely my nerves and sinews will never so hurt me again.

The flight staggers off parade to drop bonelessly into bed; and there they lie without speaking above a whisper till sleep-time, regardless of their bellies' appeal for food. Some have not faced the stripping off socks and trousers since we began our drills. Whereas for me the square is not so harsh as that former labour. Sitting to artists taught me to be still for three quarters of an hour at once, and the military positions are less

123

severe than studio poses. I have been tired, of course, dog-tired; but not drained right out. Even I've limped the other fellows' errands, half a dozen times, to Y.M. or coffee-stall, for wads and mess-tins of tea. They are too sorely demoralised to attack those few score yards of grass or gravel. Strange, heartening, heady to find myself not the feeblest here.

Our Sergeant Jenkins went down with griping pains, the first morning he had charge of us. Jenkins seemed a foul-mouthed, confident, kindly Welshman. Upon his going our flight became a job-lot, hacked out for the day to this one or that of the specialist instructors—whoever can be best-spared from his proper technicality: and these revenge on our guiltless bodies their misemployment. They have put us into maudlin fear, to moral abasement. A little longer as prey for every snapping dog upon the square, and we're hospital cases. Five have slunk there already: or rather three have slunk, and two decent lads were carried in.

I have been before at depots, and have seen or overseen the training of many men: but this our treatment is rank cruelty. While my mouth is yet hot with it I want to record that some of those who day by day exercise their authority upon us, do it in the lust of cruelty. There is a glitter in their faces when we sob for breath; and evident through their clothes is that tautening of the muscles (and once the actual rise of sexual excitement) which betrays that we are being hurt not for our good, but to gratify a passion. I do not know if all see this: our hut is full of innocents, who have not been sharpened by my penalty of witnessing:—who have not laid their wreath of agony to induce:—the orgasm of man's vice.

But they know there is more in this severity than training. Lawful discipline would not have scared them into the present funk, which with exactness of adjective we call piddling. Sit a moment on some bed in the hut, and your nose will tell you how the fellow's been: see us pack, a half-dozen at once, into the latrines three minutes before the next parade. Another week and the R.A.F. will have confirmed the coward in every one of us.

Am I overdone, emotional? Is it only the impact of strenuous conditions upon a frame unfitted by nature and its career for present hardship? It may be that there is nothing on the barrack square which can injure a wholesome man. I do not swear the contrary. Perhaps:—but recollect I am coming through easier than my companions. Alone of the hut I've energy at this moment to protest. If time has made me more worn than them, also it has made me deeper. Man's emotions, like water-plants, sprout far-rooted from his basic clay pushfully into the light. If very luxuriant they dam life's current. But these fellows' feelings, because of their youngness, seem like shallops on a river, splashly important, but passing without trace, leaving their surface clean, weedless, purling over the sunlit stones. Whereas to root out one of my thoughts—what upstirring of mud, what rending of fibre in the darkness!

I am not frightened of our instructors, nor of their overdriving. To comprehend why we are their victims is to rise above them. Yet despite my background of achievement and understanding, despite my willingness (quickened by a profound dissatisfaction with what I am) that the R.A.F. should bray me and re-mould me after its pattern: still I want to cry out that this our long-drawn punishing can subserve neither beauty nor use.

125

2

THE FOUR SENSES

Again, after breakfast, the chief instructor delivered us over to Sergeant Poulton, whom already we had found our worst tormentor. Day-long my eyes had apprehensively watched him pick on first one and then another of the flight, playing with them for an hour, twisting the point of his contempt slowly into their tenderness. This morning I developed a hollow sense that my turn was due. Each time I looked up, some part of me seemed the target of his hot gaze. Hot eyes he had and a biting trick. Sometimes his knuckles, sometimes his nails. If not, it would be the little crescents of transparent skin alongside the finger nails. These he would chew savagely, his hatchet face screwed up in rage against his fingers.

He did not actually start on me till after his practical demonstration, when it was time for questions. Then he made a fool of me, as is too easy for an instructor with a stammering recruit. Some sense of discipline ties me, tongue-ties me. He drenched my eventual dumbness with all the foul and hurtful names in his mouth: but they seemed not to soak through to the quick of my notice. I hung there more curiously miserable than indignant.

Dickson from the rear rank counselled me in an urgent whisper: 'Answer him back, Cough-drop, answer him. He sees you stuck there like a cunt, shitting yourself, and that makes him go on. Blind him with science same's you do us in the hut' . . . where among my peers I hold my own in verbal rallies. But when I am standing to attention this obscure respect for duty intervenes.

I fear the sight of me miserably squirming to dodge the goad does inflame Sergeant Poulton. 'Look at me!' he yells: but I can't. If I am angry, I can outface a man; but when this hyena curses me I sicken with shame wondering if my authority, in the past, so deflowered myself and those under me. 'Look at me, look me in the face, you short-arsed little fuck-pig,' he is yelling again. If I meet his eyes for more than a moment, my sight reels giddily outward, and my focus loses itself in a guttering rim of tears. But for that my body's swaying would throw me down. 'Well, I'm fucked, the ignorant queenie' (of our adjectives, printable or unprintable, 'ignorant' is gauged the hurtfullest). 'Funks looking at me, an' thinks his equipment's right. Blood like fucking gnat's piss.'

It may be an infirmity of my eyes, that they cannot be intensely concentrated for more than a moment. Yet my other senses share their fate. Take hearing. Out of most concerts I get one or two or three exquisite moments when myself goes suddenly empty, the entire consciousness taking flight into space upon these vibrations of perfect sound. Each time lasts an instant only: more, and I should die, for it holds still my breath and blood and vital fluid. Just so the ecstasy of a poem lies in the few words here and there—an affair of seconds.

Sound momentary: sight momentary: smell? Why, a minute after our personality returns home from an absence, we do not even smell ourselves. Touch? I do not know. I fear and shun touch most, of my senses. At Oxford the select preacher, one evening service, speaking of venery, said, 'And let me implore you, my young friends, not to imperil your immortal souls upon a pleasure which, *so I am credibly informed,* lasts less than one and three-quarter minutes.' Of direct experience I cannot speak, never having been tempted so to peril my mortal soul: and six out of ten enlisted fellows share my ignorance, despite their flaming talk. Shyness and a wish to be clean have imposed chastity on so many of the younger airmen, whose life spends itself and is spent in the enforced celibacy of their blankets' harsh embrace. But if the perfect partnership, indulgence with a living body, is as brief as the solitary act, then the climax is indeed no more than a convulsion, a razor-edge of time, which palls so on return that the temptation flickers out into the indifference of tired disgust once a blue moon, when nature compels it.

By general rumour troops are accused of common lechery and much licence. But troops are you and me, in uniform. Some make a boast of vice, to cover innocence. It has a doggy sound. Whereas in truth, with one and another, games and work and hard living so nearly exhaust the body that few temptations remain to be conquered. Report accuses us of sodomy, too: and anyone listening into a hut of airmen would think it a den of infamy. Yet we are too intimate, and too bodily soiled, to attract one another. In camps all things, even if not public, are publicly known: and in the four large camps of my sojourning there have been five fellows actively beastly. Doubtless their natures tempted others: but they fight its expression as the normal airman fights his desire for women, out of care for physical fitness.

3

OFFICERS, PLEASE

P.T. this morning was severe, especially as the daily harrowing makes us all cannibals of our nerves. The dawn gloom hindered us, by being more chill than usual. As a rule, the first P.T. makes only one or two casualties. Today seven men of the muster fell out or fainted where they ran. It is good luck to be behind a man who faints: you and the next fellow lift him, and carry him to the edge of the square, with great parade of effort. If he's decently slow in reviving, he'll save you from the rest of the period.

The omnipotence of the non-commissioned officers here in the Depot still strikes me as un-English and unfortunate. They totally eclipse the officers. We are supposed to have a flight-lieutenant over us. I saw one, when the Sergeant Major ran me: but our sergeant and corporal do not know his name or face. Probationary officers spring up like mushrooms on the square each Sunday, for Church Parade. They give the wrong orders, which our corporals correct sotto-voce for our right performance: and they are cursed before us by Stiffy, the Drill-Adjutant, our ring-master. We hear rumours that he (whose prerogative is drill) .wants to make the Depot all drill, and will not permit other officers to learn the men, or men the officers.

129

However it is, there's a complete lack of touch. No single officer has yet spoken voluntarily to a man of us. Yet to know the troops' mentality and nature and outlook is a main part of their duty. The Commandant may say they would lower themselves, if they met us. If he's so apprehensive for them, they are not the right stuff. On ceremonial, now, they are ridiculous, when they first force us into error, and then 'chew our balls off.' The corporals grumble that good officers have depth enough not to bawl about but these poor figure-heads get no practice in command. Good officers are easily made out of good material, by trying. They lose no caste as they publicly learn. A decent officer can go down on all fours among his decent men, without demeaning himself: and all men are decent till they have proved otherwise.

We have a craving for these, our natural masters. Won't they prove a different creation? We think to serve them without the reservations which apply to Stiffy, who is clay of our clay. So far the only upper being we have met (most of us in our lives) is the school-master here, who has won our golden approbation. The rough end of the hut tries to copy the accent he displays when he reads our nominal roll. It's an Oxfordy drawl, which sounds queer with Fane's East End consonants.

From the class of officer whom we'd like to serve, but whom we find asses during their weekly appearance on ceremonial, we all except Stiffy. We have for him a technical admiration, for his superb competence in drill; and he believes so earnestly that drill is as useful and natural as sunshine, that the force of his belief half converts us.

As man and character he seems not to reach his standing in drill-mastery, for a hastiness lets him swear at us on parade. 'You damned men' . . . . *you men* alone had damned the Commandant. Cursing fellows forbidden to look resentful (an airman could be charged with dumb insolence if his face glowered), fellows whose hearts are so set on obedience that they blush to feel resentful, is a sergeant-majorish trick which good corporals would not allow themselves on a formal occasion. Of course sergeant majors are lost souls, ex officio: but we feel that officers should practise dignity.

In the midst of a quiet period on square, suddenly the instructors will burst into fury, blackguarding us fore and aft. Then we guess that Stiffy has prowled up behind us to oversee. We instantly get nerves and worsen our performance. By nature the corporals are near us in feeling (there's no corporals' mess to subtract their living hours from our lives), and if let alone, they'd be patient and painstaking. But they have their promotions to earn, and the tradition is that a hot manner, brittle and painsgiving, earns the adjutant's approval.

Most mistakes on square rise out of nervousness. By straining we overshoot or undershoot the order. Once our solid Corporal Jackson got cursed by Stiffy for a fault of the squad in front. He took it dutifully. We trembled for a castigation, when we were next alone together: but in the afternoon he was equable as ever, saying, 'I won't take it out of you irks just because my bollocks were chewed to arse-paper at dinner-time.' Jackson's instruction is a running-fire of 'Swing your arms, hold your heads up, keep your dressing, keep your step, left, left, LEFT, I tell you. March by the right. Swing them up now.' So many exhortations that none of them find targets. Every drill-correction should have a man's name in it: any squad-name will do so long as you pepper them about. When we do something very bad, Jackson chuckles richly, in a stage-manner.

After his unjust Monday abuse of the Corporal, Stiffy relented and forgave us our boot-inspection penalty parade. Instead he stood us at ease on Wednesday morning and told us,

131

loudly smiling, how he'd been cursed himself and had been thirty years an instructor and these things were part of the secret of smartness. We were picked men from all the nation: drill would make us look like it and be proudly remarkable for carriage.

He was genial; we laughed whenever he smiled: but the turn clashed with his 'square' sobriety. One or other manner is insincere. I fancy that today's used to be the man's reality, before tradition and hide-bound stupidity rusted a brain which had a native bent towards drill-mania. But the others think the manual is his soul's confession of faith. He little suspects how we'd shudder, if his words came true. We pray, even in our sleep, to avoid the parade-manner, off-parade. The permanent and terrible disability of long service is that, even in plain clothes, its victims are stamped as old soldiers. Old sailors escape it; and, we hope, old airmen. There seems nothing, in legitimate air-forcing, to difform a man's body.

4

NON-COMMISSIONED OFFICERS

'You're a fool,' said the Corporal, viciously. 'Now then, what are you?'

Snaggletooth stood solid.

'Do as you're told. Say, "I'm a bloody fool, Corporal." ' Hardy was screaming now, hopping up and down on his tiny feet. Snaggle remained stock-still, saying not a word, and Hardy had to retreat by telling off poor Lofty, who asks always for kicking and is such easy meat that it's like kicking a woman. He flops in the ranks like a spare part of the squad.

Corporal Hardy took over (assistant) supervisor of our flight yesterday, from splay-footed Corporal Jackson. He'll sleep in the hut, and look after us on square, for what should be alternating periods with our permanent sergeant. But Jenkins is yet ill, and we are driven from pillar to post. I regret Corporal Jackson, who in his few days shaped to dominate us only less than Abner, but very differently. Abner was strong and not human with us. Jackson could laugh and talk, while remaining a stranger and our boss. He had had nineteen years in the ranks, and was tolerantly awaiting the corporal's-pittance of a pension, which cheapens his required wages outside the force, and so makes job-finding easier.

Hardy we knew to be slack and dirty, and tyrannical by fits.

On parade he will march us to the far end of the square, and stand us at ease for a lecture on the finer points of drill. The lecture is in his head, learned by rote, and we hear tags of it whenever Stiffy turns our way. 'When I sez "one" you tear them off your shoulders. No, no, not like that. Christ, man, if I was so big as you I'd eat my rifle:—eat it, an' shit a field gun.' For the rest it's dirty stories, which he tells us with a mirthless laugh. We must echo the lecherous noise (you can tell the smutty laugh a mile off) and mimic his lippy smile, or be bullied off our feet. Poor choices.

'Ten-a-penny N.C.O.s,' we call the corporals. They borrow half-dollars off us recruits: easily, for on fatigue-parades in the evening after instruction they select the men for the duties; and to be marked as disobliging is to sweat your guts out nightly on insensate labour. If only four of them are thus venal, the immunity of those few taints the rest. For our part we carefully humour everyone in authority: laugh at their jokes, jump to their orders. In return they moderate to us the upper tyranny—Stiffy's lightnings. That great figure ramps over the square like a man three-quarters through a boys' pack, showering out extra drills, and scaring every squad into dislocation.

His booked victims look crushed always; and are crushed, if they happen to be 'out' with their instructors. But your corporal debtor guards you from extra drill, however Stiffy may rave and sentence you, however often your name is shouted. Likewise for ready cash we may usually smile (discreetly) at the sergeants' threats to bash us. Only for this money system our life would be bad. Poulton, who's incorruptible, took James, a man half his weight, to the gym last night and battered him sore with the gloves. Then Poulton also knocks his wife about.

Today Stiffy ordered me a haircut. That meant clippers all

over, and I fell in, hating myself, outside the orderly room at five-fifteen for punishment parade. But Sergeant Lawton jeered me away. 'Bugger off, lad. There's more fucking cheese on your knob than hair on your block. Drop your slacks and flash it.' I laughed, not very gladly.

My fairness is a misfortune. Stiffy hates white faces and fair heads: such fellows are always catching his eye, and then his anger: and he has not the self-control of a rutting camel. We recruits stand together in the ranks with whispered adjurations: and help swing the clumsy ones round in turns and wheels. Ex-army fellows like Snaggle and me are useful at this, for our book-knowledge tells us what's happening, and how: but when Stiffy breaks loose the rest can't pull me through. My calm goes, and the rifle quavers out of time in my grip.

After dusk tonight Flight-Sergeant Crowe came to the hut and asked me for Raleigh's History of the Air during the war. It's a popular book, and another fellow had borrowed it: so he was unlucky. He gazed at my shelf and wanted to know if I'd studied psychology: and what were the best books to help him write a paper on the psychology of an airman. Would Foyle's keep that sort? If he paid my fare would I run up on Saturday and buy them for him? He'd get me a pass to London.

Also why was I in the R.A.F.? I explained that I'd overdone the imaginative life, as expressed in study, and needed to lie fallow awhile in the open air. That meant earning a living by my hands, as I had no resources, and my scholarly hands weren't worth a meal at any trade. So I had enlisted. I spared him my urge downwards, in pursuit of the safety which can't fall further: and the necessary compulsion to re-learn poverty, which comes hard after some years of using money. I reckon I've got my wishes, so far as being bottom-dog and poor are concerned: but perhaps few doctors would have prescribed Hardy or Sergeant Poulton as a remedy for nerves.

5

MY HOURS

The Depot for me remains a moon-haunted memory:
for the moon-rays break into our glass box of a hut night after
night through some one of the four window-ranks and possess
its air. It is marvellous to walk directly from the fug of man into
chilly open silence: especially on nights rich with cloud, when
the moon, very high, shines down through a casement of this
sky-drapery, narrowing its light to just my part of the earth, as
it were a room.

However tired the work has left me, I cannot sleep a whole
night away: not once since my enlistment. The dark hours
march by me, and I lie half-indifferent to them, not particularly
wanting to sleep, but still less wanting to think consecutively,
or attend to the hut-sounds: for our hut persists in being a main
intruder upon what should be mental peace. After midnight my
head jars at every vibration across the still air:—fellows dream
vocally of girls, muttering their pet names aloud: or shortly
moan, 'Don't, don't' (the day-long complainant grumble of the
service man is his night-habit too: mutely he begs always for
pity, having no self-defence). They sigh and fart, amid the
piano janglings of their wire beds—and reveille shatters the end

of the night like a last exasperation, just when I have sunk into the custom of lying still. I think I've heard every reveille since that first day in camp.

So the appellant moon easily conjures me outside, into its view. Dressing is the affair of a moment: gym shoes and trousers, with my shirt already on. Sharply the keen air refreshes the stubbled roundness of my head. If only the powers would realise how they dull their men's sensitiveness of reception, by having our hair clipped too short for the wind to play with. I slouch meditatively, my head ever forward, eyes on the ground, to give my negligent feet unconscious warning of obstacles. Wits inwardly turned cannot watch a man's path.

Once after two in the morning the guard-reliefs picked me up. Their corporal half-shouted at me: and my spring of fright, when he too-suddenly broke into my notice, shook him to rueful laughter. 'Can't you sleep, boy?' he asked. I replied that I was walking just for fun. 'Well, go to bed: I wish *I* fucking well could.' The rough kindness of his tone was as simple and direct as the night air. Poor people achieve this intimate contact in voice more easily than the compartmented rich.

I wandered the other way, to avoid his further kindness, and fetched up at the laundry gate. Its solitary sentry concluded I had toothache. When I said not, his imagination leaped to the other physical cause. It was Thursday: I was broke and hungry. He pulled me two pennies from his pocket, and forced them against my reluctance. 'Get yourself a cha,' he insisted gently, and opened his gate for me to reach the coffee-stall at the crossroads. 'Go on, mate: it's jonnuk. I'm on till four, and will let you in. Bloody binding to fuck round this cunting fence all night.'

Another time the sergeant of the guard sent his runner to collect me, and asked if I knew that night-walking was forbidden. I said I understood not, on the roads. He shifted ground. It was uncommon. I admitted, dryly, that I'd noticed few doing it tonight. He smiled, and more dryly still begged me not to walk up and down too near the sentries, as my footfalls kept them awake! At the first greyness in the sky, or just before, I'd return to the hut. When I edged the creaking door open, inch by inch, the slow warm breathing of the fellows would pulse out to my ears, as though a huge beast were stabled there in the blackness.

6

INTEMPERATE

More Poulton. This has been an awful day. The morning was just average bad: but through the afternoon hours, a muggy, sweating afternoon, he slowly tightened his pressure on us. Some display was preparing in the gym, and this cancelled our second P.T. The fellows regretted it: they like the gym, which leaves my heart hammering one hundred and ten to the minute; while my breathing gets so forced from exhaustion that it pries my mouth distressfully half-open: and anything like a meal for the next hour turns my stomach sick. Usually I wait till six o'clock, and then have a mug of the warm wash-like tea of the canteen, with two tuppenny wads. Contrarily I half-enjoy the drilling, which tires out the others. I have to thank my past life for the power to 'stay put' indefinitely.

When the tea trumpet sounded Sergeant Poulton was almost at his worst. We were jaded in mind and body. An angry instructor makes miserable men, and a miserable squad flops like a wet dish-cloth. Individuals may be doing their best, but there is no ensemble.

Perfection of drill resides not in individual perfections: nor would fifty of the best men in a new squad drill well. Smartness depends on knowing the man in front, and the man behind, and   139 those on each side. All must bring down their left heels simultaneously, with a slightly-marked beat to keep time with a metronome in the brain. This comes with time, after training. It can only be done by a mind absolutely serene. It's a matter of trust, of unconscious certainty to tell you what right and left are going to do. Then all the feet will clash as one, and the flight be a flight, and not fifty men.

After six hours' rough handling we could not be like that. Poulton insisted. The trumpets went on calling. He set his teeth. 'No tea for you skunks today. I'll keep you here all night.' He had not seen Stiffy, the Drill-Adjutant, approaching from his rear, to learn why one squad was delayed in dismissal. Stiffy called the Sergeant, endured a low explanation, and replied loudly for us to hear. 'Put them on again at five-fifteen, and let them have it.' So we fell in again after half an hour, knowing we were to be crucified.

Some of the rear rank were heard muttering, as Poulton checked us off. 'Pack that up,' he snarled, 'else you'll all be in the guard-room. I'll break your bastard hearts.' He began to double us up and back, with many quick turns. Any man's mistake communicated itself to all behind him: so we fell into confusion. Poulton bared his gums at us in rage, like a dog, and sent us to the hut for full packs and rifles.

This is punishment-kit, and greatly increases the severity of quick drill. He weighted the load to the utmost of his power, by often pulling us suddenly to the halt, as we ran. This is the rankest collar-work, each single artificial pound eating up tissue to start or stop it instantaneously. The cross-straps sawed into our shoulders, and the rifle, banging loosely with the spring of each running stride, bruised cruelly my four-times broken, knotty collar-bone. Each time anyone faulted Poulton stopped the lot, to repeat the movement.

The lights flicked on, all down one side of the drill-ground. The Sergeant took us over there to have us in plain view. The shadows filled with the other squads, wondering. After three quarters of an hour without an easy the sweat had oozed out from our shirts, through the tunics, to the cross-braced equipment whose brown-clayed texture it turned oily black in spots. My hands and knees trembled violently, my gape-mouthed breathing was surely very loud. Every so many gulps erected a catch in my throat, which ran convulsively into my lung. Then the broken rib in the wall of my chest leaped.

At last he halted us facing the big arc-lamp and stood us easy. I rubbed the sweat blindness from my eyes unsteadily, with my sleeve: and saw the vapour of my breathing pale in the dark. Poulton going down the front rank paused by me and peered, wrinkling his nose with disgust. 'When did you last have a bath?' 'Yesterday, Sergeant,' I gasped, truthfully; for every Thursday and Monday a little tea house in the village street finds me a hot bath. It costs little and feels worth all my pay. Hot water is rare in the Depot. 'Open your collar,' he ordered, thrust his hand roughly inside, against my wet breast. 'Christ, the bloody man's lousy. You and you,' to Sailor and Hoxton, others of his dislikes, 'march the filthy bugger over to the wash-house and scrub the shit out of him, properly.'

I tried to walk away between my escort, in front of everybody, as if I did not care: but any firm accusation convinces me of guilt. So soon as the doorway hid us from the crowd, I wanted to choke out something in my defence. Sailor wouldn't have a word of it. 'God,' he swore, 'if that long spunking streak of piss pokes his head in here after us, I'll knock seven different sorts of shit out of him. But, mate, you let the flight down, when he takes the mike out of you every time. Give the ignorant shit-bag a fucking great gob of your toffology.'

Next day, in the first stand-at-ease of first period:—'Short-arse, you there, Ross, what's your bleedin' monaker:—what d'you know?' Such nonplussing questions are Poulton's favourite gambit for a hazing. *Spring to attention.* 'Sergeant,' I dutifully intone. He wouldn't stop. 'I arst you a question, you little cunt.' But I am not tired at this time of day: by Sailor's advice of priggery I made to drawl out, 'Well, Sergeant, specifically of course we can know nothing—unqualified—but like the rest of us, I've fenced my life with a scaffolding of more or less speculative hypotheses.'

The rear rank deflated appreciatively, tired sounding, like the wind in wet trees. The Sergeant stared: then whispered to himself, 'Jesus fucking Christ.' At that Sailor let out a high, sudden, singing laugh. 'Flight—Attention,' Poulton yelled, and the drill went forward, gingerly. 'My Christ,' exulted James, thumping my back later, in the hut's safety, 'the silly twat didn't know if his arse-hole was bored, punched, drilled, or countersunk.'

It was the last time I was called out to make public sport. Soon after roll-call Sergeant Jenkins, rosy and round with drink, burst into our hut, and called us from bed to the one gangway. 'Fall in properly,' he hiccoughed, reeling down the floor. We lined up barelegged, in shirts, blinking the first sleep out of our eyes. 'Flight attention: right dress: as you were: right dress: as you were: right dress: jump to it: eyes front: number: move to the right in fours: form fours: right: left turn: stand at ease.'

'You're mine, tomorrow,' he roared, shaking his marching-stick at us. It was brass-pointed, split lengthwise, and hinged like a pair of callipers, to measure the infantry-pace. 'See that point? It's going up your fucking guts till it's full of blood. I mean to have three rings on it a day. Flight attention: dismiss:

no, not that way: smartly: let me hear your boot-heels click.'

'But, Sergeant, we haven't our boots on'—that was Nobby piping up. 'No boots? You bloody-fucking-cunting-syphilitic bastard. You're improperly dressed: all of you. Well, I don't care a bugger. Per ardua ad asbestos. What does that mean? All together after me, "Fuck you, Jack, I'm fireproof." On the hands down. Up, down: make the clinkers rattle round your shitty arse-holes. Keep still down there. You're like a donkey's tool: will move for anything. Now I'll tell you the story of when I drilled the W.A.A.C.s. Left leg raise: right leg raise. Haircut you, and you, and you. What yer laughing at? All right: get to bed. I'm Taff' Jenkins, and you're a damned good first-week squad. 'night everybody. Ar-r-r hyd yr N,N,N, Nos.' The beery song died away behind the falling rain.

7

A FRESH START

We are to begin again. Taffy, who'd served just before the war with Stiffy in the Guards, saw him after breakfast today and asked that we might be put back to first week. 'I'll put it right with the lads,' he promised, when Stiffy feared that it might daunt us. 'They've been properly buggered these last days.' He very bluntly told the Adjutant the harmfulness of the bullying we'd had.

Taffy's gloating over the way we are to go through it at his hands has a healthy hiccoughing laughter in its background: and we are happy enough with it to cheek him back, off parade. Then he chases us, with surprising speed for a malt-tub, and prods us with the famous stick. On drill he is a queer cat, playing with us, and we are queer individual mice: silent stifflyjerking mice, and a motionless, not at all silent, cat. The filled parade reminds me of a puppet theatre. Stiffy is a master of drill, and our ignorance his orchestra.

Four of our hospital fellows have missed the flight. They will go back to fatigues, when they are well; and four latecomers to the Depot have been advanced to make up our number. One of them is no gain: a lanky eighteen-year-old, whose legs recurve like a seal's flippers: gawky, uncooked, playful. He powders his cheeks, after scraping the thin down

144

from them with a safety razor, scents his hair, scents his teeth, stinks at the armpits and feet. Sergeant Jenkins, seeing suddenly in the ranks this pasty face and lolloping mouth smiling wetly at him, cried out, 'And who let you into my flight, Gaby?' The name stuck, Gaby proud of it.

October the twentieth was the first dawning altogether too wet for P.T. I marked the salved hour with a white memorial stone. It will save me, if this autumn should prove regularly wet. Our drills went on in a great shed near the dining hall. When, later, we scurried in overcoats down the wet road to school, the tattered elms were sighing, groaning and wheezing in a dreary wind, which was flecked and made chilly by rain. Squalls flung the drops of glittering water from these boughs in showers after our backs. We overtook a woman: so fast did we drive on that in three minutes she was eighty yards behind. 'Flight . . . about turn,' roared Taffy. Back we swung in our tracks, facing the woman. 'Eyes right.' She blushed to her eyes, too: as did some of us. 'Flight about turn.' We chased her down again.

That was yesterday and at night, half an hour after lights out, little Nobby, that honest weakly radish, pulled on his trousers, and crept from bed to the stove whose fire was yet hot, though dying. He shivered, hooked open the hinged lid, and cowered over it. Elsewhere the red coals' glowing lost itself in the bigness of the room: but their first up-light smoothed the modelling of his face, like a faun's face, where he held it between his hands, brooding (do fauns brood?) for long minutes: till I fell asleep.

8

THE TIME-TABLE

The hours are not so long: it's their tension. Every
ear strains to divine from the first syllable of each order what
the whole will be—for in no other way will our yet-deliberate
minds respond to it punctually. Every muscle must be held
tight, sinews all at stretch, back straight, head up, knees braced
back. The drill-book calls it an easy, natural uprightness. Look
at the old-soldier strut and the thick red back of his neck!

Remember to be sorry for our feet. They are unnaturally
shod with stiff boots, five pounds heavy per pair, and metal
plated underneath to click loudly on the ground. At every stride
(and recruits are made to march one-third faster than trained
men) we must bang down the heel sharply, beating the pace:
and at every turn about must lift them high, and stamp, stamp,
stamp, thrice before shooting the foot forward in the new direction. Each stamp jars up the spinal column into the brain,
which soon aches dully: while our soles burn like fire.

Then, too, in arms' drill we must strain to recover the vertical
against the unbalancing weight of the cumbersome rifle in the
hollow of the right arm or on the left shoulder. Or we must remember to grip the bodkin canes, whose slim malicious smoothness tries to slip from our cold-cramped fingers. Also they make
us shout the numbers, one-two-three-four, all in chorus as we

march or turn. This makes us feel fools and besides is difficult, for sucking our bellies in while we blow out our chest-ribs seems to paralyse the lungs. I can walk fifty miles in the day, freshly: and am done after twenty minutes' marching. Oh, life is very difficult, even with Taffy Jenkins as instructor!

We start at six forty-five for P.T. and after it dress fully, and rush to fall in for breakfast at a quarter to eight. The preliminary paradings for the meal, and ordered defile by left and right flights into mess-deck, take so long that we get only eight minutes to bolt down the food and tea, which fortunately is seldom hot. Then a run to the hut for five minutes of dressing and putting on belts and cleaning guns: and by ten minutes after eight we are fallen in for first period drill.

After a hard hour and a quarter of this they give us ten minutes' easy (just enough, on a rasping day, to meet nature's urgency. We sprint to the double-banked latrines and sprint back, dressing and undressing on the road). There follows second period till near eleven o'clock. At eleven we are due for school which is eight minutes' sharp walk-distance. Our instructors make this a demonstration march, of the strictest. So in the school hour we do not shine: we flop over the forms and gather breath for our return journey, another march-race, severer than the first, for the road now goes up-hill.

Before we get back the rest of the Depot has gone on parade for dinner. So for us it's a scamper into the hut to grab knife, fork and spoon, and away, still breathless, across the square in fours. After dinner we at last get a half-hour to ourselves. I then wash my very grubby hands.

Afternoon is like morning. A drill period: an hour and twenty minutes' hard in the gymnasium: a quarter of an hour before tea, to change our sweaty day-shirts for those in which we sleep. We'd like to change our trousers, too; the cotton bits round the waist and the pockets are clammy with wetness: but we have only the one pair. Of course their woolly parts are not cold-feeling. They smell, already.

After tea a lecture, and twice or thrice a week fire-picket with its fatigues to follow. The other nights I change hurriedly into blue (to get the illusion of fresh clothes) and catch the District Railway to Baker Street. Though my boot-soles are so thick, the feel of the London pavements through them is celestial. London is out of bounds, and a service policeman on the local platform examines our tickets as we land. I have a season from the next station down the line (a lawful place) and show him that. The station staff love the joke and help me by lies to the police. They are all ex-service men: and the services are one great union against these domestic spies. The train-conductor told me how in 1919 the late train on Saturday night would be like a public lavatory, with airmen spewing, pissing and fighting along its swaying length. Now it is quiet as a reading room, so much have we and the Air Force changed. Ordinary men and women enter our coaches, unhesitatingly.

This all sounds as though we had much spare time: but our cleaning and polishing take hours longer than they should. Recruits, who are clumsy at the job, are much more minutely inspected than serving airmen. Also they are given a harder task. The older the equipment the easier it cleans. We achieve comparative miracles with our new stiff gear, after heart-breaking expenditure of pains. Perhaps that is right. Service life holds no terror for the man who has endured the full Depot.

That Monday night, for example, when we were to suffer inspection by Stiffy on the morrow:—why the boot-cleaning came in paroxysms. Varnishes and waxes, hot and cold irons, candle-ends, the stove's warmth, hot water: some larded on a spirit polish, and burned it off with a flame: anything to get a

148

mooth shining blackness on the recalcitrant toe-caps. We all
mucked-in' together: so it was generally bitter when three
ellows failed:—at least, Stiffy was busy and postponed the
ordeal without notice; but Corporal Jackson, our equable Jack-
on, condemned these three to extra duties. It was a sad end
o a whole-hearted communism of effort.

9

SCHOOL

We had thought the rumour of school and school masters a joke: but inside the echoing room whose pitch-pine desks had little ink-splattered wells sunken along their top edge we hushed quickly, under an access of infantilism. 'There' only one thing,' says Taffy, 'that the Air Force can't do: put u in the family way.' We felt and feared, all at once, that if thi new service of ours took the whim it might put us back t pupilage, again.

The master was youngish, a lean dark civilian. Hand i pocket (what a liberty and comfort this seemed! We daren put our hands in) he stood by the dais, against the wall-map c Europe, and looked at us. We gained a little confidence. We ar Air Force ('Royal Air Force') and superior to civvy gink Gaby thought she might assert the manhood our nicknam denied her so she dropped her books and splashed ink on th master's fingers. He instantly developed sharpness. Gaby wa ordered out and came back after a minute, subdued, and hidin from us the swollen palm of his right hand. 'Serve the little sh right,' said everyone, quietening down.

Then the master spoke us fairly, in an Oxford manner. Hi pleasantness seemed earnest for us to do something for ou selves. From the first sentence my analysing mind felt a confli between his spirit and the other side of the valley. Do things for ourselves . . . over there we were taught to obey orders, and to wait for orders. Zeal was misplaced. The part of our mental anatomy most kicked by the instructors had been not our laziness but our blundering zeal to do over well. In the training camp we were being subdued to the passivity of puppets, with something of their immediacy and automatism, when master jerked our string.

Here was this other master, only just across the Pinne in M. Section, telling us that education made us worth having in the Air Force and that it flowed from the inner man, educed by his will. Wills? Airmen weren't entitled to them, were they, except to second the sergeants' wills? Where was Taff' Jenkins? He had deserted us, left us to the mercy of this new voice which went on to talk bolshevism. We had a chance, it seemed, in spare hours to better ourselves for civvy life. But civil life is half a life away: and for spare hours, we are too stupefied with square .to fill them except with sleep. This is such a spare hour and these forms not so hard as they looked. Let's hope he likes his pleasant voice and will drone on over us. As he speaks his fist coils and uncoils in his left pocket, like a snake.

No luck: he is giving out papers. We are each to write an essay on our schooling, what it was, and our aspirations, what they are. 'More blinking essays,' muttered a disappointed voice. He came round with the blank paper, and bending low said something to each of us. Doesn't he know we're a flight, not loose fellows? He's talking to us one by one. To me he said, 'What you write will not go beyond myself. I want you to give me your confidence and tell me the exact truth of what I've asked.'

Risk it? There was a suppressed interest in his voice. I took up my pen and wrote how since the age of twelve I'd helped my-

151

self with scholarships and benefits through school to a university and past a degree in history to a research fellowship in political theory. Afterwards I had wearied of abstractions and thrown up that life and enlisted: and now wanted no more intellectual knowledge, my brain being already too ingrown for the daily practicalities of Hut 4.

The hour had passed. We filed out into the corridor's silence and rent it with our vile scrapery of hobnails. Pipe in mouth Taffy sat waiting for us on the steps. We pounded wildly, heel and toe, up the hill. Ten minutes late for dinner. Odds and sods to eat. Damn all school.

The mail had come during dinner and lay distributed on our beds. In his letter there was bad news for Garner, who tore up the photographs which had stood on his locker and with his face in his blankets began to sob like a child. Real shaking sobs, which echoed across the hut like minute-guns, making it miserable. We kept clear of him till the whistle went for five minutes to parade. He washed his streaked face and fell in, saying nothing.

10

OUR INSTRUCTOR

Salacious and wholly Welsh is long-suffering Sergeant Jenkins, florid in description, florid in abuse, florid in praise. He seems not disappointed with our failures, while we are trying: and he has a fine nose for a try. His arms' drill is called as good as Flight-Sergeant (Jock) Mackay's, the chief instructor: good judges even prefer Taffy's after his fifth pint. Our flight is proud of him. 'We're Taffy's,' we tell the less fortunate recruits. Our week of torture before he came back quickens us to keep him pleased with us.

Taffy takes his own liberties. Last week at ceremonial he tramped across the hollow square to Stiffy, in command. At the regulation distance he halted with the regulation halt and saluted with a perfection that thrilled.

'Permission to fall out, Sir!'

'Why, Sergeant?'

'To visit the Sergeants' Mess, Sir.'

'What for, Sergeant?'

Taffy exploded. 'A drink, Sir.' Stiffy staggered a pace, and gave way.

'Take that man's name, Sergeant,' yells Stiffy another time, 'the tall fellow in the rear rank.' 'Taken it, Sir.' 'Well then take it again': for Stiffy loves his old mate, and they exchange their

153

time-consecrated gags across the parade ground. 'That long man of yours, still, Sergeant Jenkins. He's lazy; he's not trying. Give him an extra drill.' 'Got him, Sir.' 'The man's a bloody fool, Sergeant. Give him two drills.' 'Keep him on all night, Sir.' Breakdown of Stiffy and the tension.

Lofty of course got no extra drill at all. Taffy does not believe in established punishments. A hobnailed gallop, screaming, down the wet road, three or four bruising jabs with the stick of office. . . . These in his judgment do us good and leave no rancour over the week-end. We respect his keenness upon our account so that we'd take much beating from him. 'Extra drills,' he snorts; 'if you've spare spunk for five more minutes than I've given you by tea-time, then post me to the Boy Scouts.' And I think he does honestly run us about as empty, each day, as is good for a flight's courage.

There aren't many instructors like Taffy. Most of them itch to put their mouths upon subjects of instruction and cannot keep from biting one another, downward in degree; even they bite their juniors' squads with a great voice of holy authority. This is bad for the earth-worms, for us upon the ground: ours is the residual resentment, as beings too poor to turn. Our revenge has to be taken behind their backs, fearfully, in curses, ridicule or parody. The man sharpest bitten will be loudest in anger: his friends silent on his behalf: while the others make the affair one more impersonal item in the general account. Good-humouredly, though. We enlisted expecting few but evil-smelling bouquets.

'March?' Sergeant Jenkins would wail. 'A set of filleted crabs: and if I tell 'em to shout, it's ruptured they are, like anæmic parrots. O God, what did I do to deserve such a mob?' He banged his head back against the quivering hut-door and dissolved in sham tears, for he'd seen Stiffy coming. 'The damned rotten thing about it is, Sir, that they drill bloody fine when they think I'm not looking. Turn your back, Sir,' and round spun Taffy himself to shout over the drill manual at us while he and Stiffy listened to the rattle of our performing rifles. At the end Stiffy said, 'Not so dusty: how did it sound to you, Sergeant Jenkins?' 'If you ask me, Sir,' replied Taffy unabashed, 'like a pack of skeletons frigging on a tin roof.'

Yet we cannot be really proud of Taffy's pride in our bolshevism when we know in our hearts that we are any sergeant's to be knocked about in silence. Some of us cravenly admit this feebleness and moan about it in lack of shame. Others try, by making their impulse supplement the directing impulse, to retain a fig of voluntariness. They 'will' right turn when the sergeant says right turn, and so on. A pitiful pretence of a soul-salve, that, in my judgment, and a corruption of discipline. The good soldier is inconsequential as a child.

11

NOW AND THEN

Things are indeed gentler for us. Tonight even there was a revival of sky-larking in the hut, prolonged after lights out by three irresponsibles, one of whom owned Fane's shriking Cockney voice. Admirable in such unruly energy after the hard day. However, tomorrow we'll all help pay for it; the orderly sergeant banged into the hut on his return from staff parade and hushed us rudely. That means a collective report, and the hatefulness of being punished. What attracted him as much as the noise was our flaring chimney. Fane had piled coal on the stove just at ten o'clock (when, orders say, fires are to be drawn) and now its red top is clattering and its red pipe roaring with the forcible flames. By their changing light I'm note-making, very late, but without comment: for my sleeplessness has become a hut-joke.

They are wrong who imagine that troops today are violent livers. They take nothing soberly enough for that. Twenty years ago—or seventeen years, my limit of direct experience—they were indeed brutal. Then every incident ended in dispute and every dispute either in the ordeal of fists (a forgotten art, today) or in a barrack-court-martial whose sentences were too often mass-bullying of anyone unlike the mass. Of one unit little stronger than our flight I cannot remember a parade during three months without a discoloured eye. Usually five or six men bore fighting damages. This R.A.F. is a girls' school beside it.

Even our manners are very good:—if our base labelling of one another be discounted. It is not rude when you call him a bloody cunt, upon no grounds at all. He'll only throw lying bastard at you, back. These stingless forms of speech are the free-trade of equals. My fastidious throat chokes over oaths and obscenities: therefore I cannot speak very friendly to their ears: and my not answering them in kind debars them from cursing me. So in small-talk (which besides I've never had) there's an artificial constraint between us. I hate being helped and make their helping me an ungrateful labour. Yet with these exceptions we're on a level and understanding friendship. I find in them an answering male-kindness and natural spark, which makes me curiously safe with them. To live in Hut 4 is to have the feet on solid earth.

Our tangible life has a muscled nudity, joined to such candour of impulse as would (were it coherent, deliberate and expressed) properly be called absolute. But it is dumb. The hut's speech-range is Saxon, and abstract words come from their lips rare and uneven, stinking of print. I suspect that these fluent gestures, the variety of tone, their ceaseless extravagances of body flow in part from verbal poverty and relieve just those emotions which sophisticated man purges, uttered or unuttered, into phrase.

We use each other's things, if we have need, without asking leave. That is common sense. He does my toothbrush no harm that can be felt or seen or smelt: and what other criteria exist? After Tuesday and the emptiness of all pockets, anyone with week-end relics of cigarettes or coppers shares them out naturally or sees them shared. After pay-time on Friday a return is

157

made; more or less, as regards cigarettes: exactly, as regards money. There is no begging: no need for it. Who dare refuse when it may be his necessity next week? In the repayment of a money loan there is charming shyness and punctuality. The precise sum is slipped into your hand, while your eyes and his sedulously avoid meeting or seeing it.

Half-inching is venial, in certain lines of goods:—issues articles, cleaning gear, sealed-pattern equipment, or consumable stores, like soap. Personal kit is borrowed with the high hand (till found out) but not stolen. The victim stamps about raging and the assistance covers him with loud noises of horror —every man of it, except the guilty one, enviously meaning to do the same tomorrow if he can. Yet you help yourself only to fill a deficiency, not to hoard. It's a question of making use. Also none of us has any property we love.

12

STOCK-TAKING

When you are very fit, square is only the hardest work: but if you are the least bit less than well it is very, very painful, a torture drawn out day after day till you grow better or succumb. The square holds all our life now. We do not see the wintry river, the bare trees, and the camp's country quietness.

Even for me, her chief servant, the moon is finished. She has not shined so brightly just of late: it has rained and wet clothes are a penalty to hut-dwellers: it has been too cold for loitering and only in leisure can a man appreciate his moon. But these are excuses only. The reason is that we now live for drill with arms and foot-drill and ceremonial and P.T. You'll see us practising movements after roll-call, in stockinged feet, between the beds. Our talk is of training: we have lost all private views. Only in the evenings we are sometimes merry, and always noisy, round the hut-stoves which we make to glow hotly with storm-wood and stolen coal. But too many go to sleep at eight o'clock out of weariness.

In our chatter we still speak hopefully of the R.A.F. as a prospect, assuming that Depot is an ordeal which earns liberty for unchased work, ahead. It must be better ahead for England's flying would be bankrupt, now, if all her airmen wasted

159

all their time, like us. The laboured nerve-strain of the constant supervision and checking and abuse and punishment of squad-life has ironed the last eagerness out of us: or rather has covered it, for I suspect that essentially we retain our inbred selves and secretly remember our dreams.

Nobby is miserable. We keep him company, afraid that he wishes to destroy himself. Lofty talks of being bought out, for he is too physically loose to control his arms and legs in drill and so is always under punishment. Six are in hospital: but the forty others are of an undaunted sturdiness. We hang together, trustily, except over the dividing of food at table. Then hunger intervenes: and airmen fall easily to its mistrust, having been mostly poor with the poverty which breeds ungenerous suspicion. Most of us unconsciously favour ourselves when we are dividing: unless I'm on and I consciously serve myself short. No virtue there. Like the Lady of Shalott I prefer my world backwards in the mirror.

We grumble at the food, and those grumble loudest who have never before had enough to eat, and that little also ill-cooked. Such grumbles are part of our universal pretence towards past gentility. Really the raw food is excellent and the cooking what airmen deserve. We wolf our food-lumps too runningly to taste a flavour. So also those who enlisted in rags do most complain of the ill-cut and shoddy uniform: while others of us think it wonderful that anyone should reckon us worth dressing free. Fane has turned himself into our hut tailor (his father and mother deal in worn clothes), and for a weekly tariff which suits our pay he creases everybody's trousers with the knife-edge that Stiffy demands.

Our talks are of the pictures or of football cups and leagues; when they are not of shop. That day the Coalition fell I lay and listened till lights out, to hear much of Chelsea Arsenal, but never a word of Lloyd George. Sometimes (and it's best then) men will bandy the arcana of their trades; fitters and electricians are nearly incomprehensible but so keenly alive as to be infective, like Jew traders chaffering in Yiddish.

The very succinct existence wakens opposite cravings. They come fingering my books, yearning over the foreign ones as some cypher that would make them rich. To my relatively-educated judgment they bring little problems of religion and natural history and science. I find pathos in these unthinking and unthought difficulties: but as regularly they frighten me with the bed-rock sureness of their opinions' background. An idea (as of the normality of marriage, which gives the man a natural, cheap, sure and ready bed-partner), if they have grown up with it, has become already, at their age of twenty, enthroned and unchallengeable, by mere use. They prefer supine belief to active doubt.

Still the key of Hut 4 remains laughter: the laughter of shallow water. Everywhere there's the noise of games, tricks, back-chat, advices, helps, councils, confidences, complaints: and laughs behind the gravest of all these. The noise is infernal. Our jazz band is very posh of its kind, because Madden leads it with his mandoline. He is supported by two coal-pans, the fire buckets, five tissued combs, two shovels, the stove doors, five locker lids and vocal incidents. The louder it is the louder they sing, the more they leap about their beds, strike half-arm balances, do hand-springs and neck-rolls, or wrestle doggily over the floors and iron-bound boxes. There's hardly a night without its mirthful accident of blood-letting.

13

THE LITTLE MORE

Today opens our third week on square; everybody and everything tightens on us. Taffy gave us warning that we'd be for it if Stiffy caught a glimpse of clumsiness or hesitation henceforward in our motions. Corporal Hemmings had taken us for the dawn P.T. We slacked with him, and not we only. The whole body of recruits has a dislike for him and, when he commands, the entire parade goes listless. We dislike him enough to be keener on earning his curses than his praise.

Stiffy came across during first period and put us through a racing performance of nearly all the drill manual. 'They're a very promising lot,' he told the Sergeant, afterwards, apart. That a hint of praise might not spoil our trying, he kept his face and manner from all sign of satisfaction. When his eye first swept along our flight, it filled suddenly. He sent Garner and myself back into the rear rank, and warned Sergeant Jenkins there'd be trouble if any pale-headed men were seen in the front again. 'White hair, white liver,' he said. 'Those are the first sort of chaps to run in a scrap.' During his ten minutes eighteen names were booked for extra drills. Of course we do not do them; but Stiffy, not knowing that, went off rubbing his hands at the good morning. We delayed to rub ours till he was out of sight.

I was entertaining a sharp dose of malaria and most of the day passed hazily. Apparently I stumbled and shambled through. My neighbours each side would see to that and the rear rank is cushy. Corporal Hardy is very short and cannot watch it without stretching a-tiptoe. Nor was he caring, today, about our correctness. He was angry because Stiffy had told him off for drilling us always in the far arm of the parade ground where the cook-house buildings hid us from sight.

At three o'clock he was in more trouble for keeping the flight ten minutes overtime on musketry. He saluted and yelled, 'Yes, Sir,' with loud joy as for a favour when Stiffy swore he'd put him on the report. Five minutes later as we were marching out towards the gymnasium across the empty square, the Corporal gave an explosive 'Eyes right' to Stiffy remotely descried behind the notice-board away up on the main road. This was open cheek: but Hardy had tried that morning to resign his stripes, in an effort to escape the Depot where life pinched him after the affair of Benson. The Adjutant would not grant him either posting or reversion and Hardy's out for mischief.

The next thing I remembered was Cook's waking me up, where I lay in bed sweating under about seven men's blankets. The hut lights were on and he had brought me a tin of tea and a hot sausage roll. 'Scran up!' he called in his sailor's belling tone against my ear, which buzzed for minutes after.

'What's all this in aid of?' I asked, stupidly.

'Well, you're a bit crabbed-like, mate.' He scratched his cheek.

'And the time?'

'It's gone rounds, long ago.' Three minutes later went Last Post. Sailor came over to borrow my Don Quixote, an excuse to sit on the bed and ask if I were going sick in the morning. The shivers of my fever had frightened everybody. Sailor had

163

been one of the gang who had undressed me after gym, which, it seems, I'd got through without comment from the instructor.

What troubles me there when I'm well is partly a physical repugnance (I hate cozening my body, even by order) and partly fear. The question I set myself as often as I think of it and now we have P.T. twice daily is not whether I'll break down at it, but when. This breaking point is always within reach; and some day my distaste will conquer me and strike. The nervous anticipation of that moment waits for me round every corner and is breaking me. Physically I'm good enough to down any man of my weight in the hut. Only they love P.T. as I loathe it. They feel and flex their lithe bodies, even in spare hours, for delight in them.

14

CEREMONY

The drill programme has been changed. We do P.T. in the first afternoon period, on top of dinner: and the rest of the time is to be spent on ceremonial. Stiffy is preparing for the Cenotaph Service next month: Depot always provides the R.A.F. contingent to line its bit of Whitehall while Kings and Princes lay wreaths: the recruits, they say, are smarter on parade than serving airmen whose drill-training may lie years behind them in forgetfulness.

Our sergeant is angry at this new programme. He finds the routine three-months' course just enough to ground his squads thoroughly in drill (of which after all we do only five hours daily: the rest is school and signalling and lectures) and the effect of cenotaph practice is to torpedo all ordinary instruction. We, the raw material, waste no tears on that.

Corporal Hemmings again supervised the gymnasium-work today. He slave-drove us as usual: and again the flight was mulish and hung together, so his rage blunted itself on a ring of bowed backs and found no particular victim. He is new at his job and knows few exercises: instead he repeats each three times over to fill his hour and a quarter; and gives no easies so that the chief instructor may never see his men lolling about.

P.T. ended: but Corporal Hardy was not at the gym door

to march us back to the hut. When he's away Sailor sometimes takes over the flight. He clowns it well with us in his commands: —orders 'Guys stiffen' for Attention and 'Twos into fours git': —traditional relics of the American army in France. Perhaps the root of Sailor's voice is not so much laughter as delight in living. Some madness of joy seems to take us whenever he marches us about. But he may do it only after Stiffy's gone: at tea-time and at night.

So we waited five minutes for the corporal, who was behind the canteen. He came out wiping his mouth. We told him how late it was and he doubled us at one run the five hundred yards to the hut. This came a little heavy upon us, just after P.T. and in marching boots. The other flights had already fallen in for the ceremonial: we hastily draped the puttees round our legs, snatched equipment and rifles and dashed after them. Stiffy punished us for being late by another double, fully equipped as we were, to the main gate and back. Need everyone take a pleasure in kicking our mute inglory?

The parade was an awful show but the stoutness of the band-master gave it a relieving moment. Stiffy was discontented with our first pace, which the opening crash of the band should stimulate to a complete stride. 'Try it again, Bandmaster. It's not right.' The apprehensive-eyed first Sergeant Major, standing woefully behind Stiffy, echoed him. 'Try it again, Bandmaster.' His final syllables pealed into the treble, like Welsh lamentations.

'NO—THAT—WON'T—DO!' roared Stiffy for the second time, punctuating each word with an angry stamp. The Sergeant Major unfolded his long wooden legs and ran to lend the bandmaster his two extra arms, to help conduct the music. The great running feet, like floats at the end of fishing-lines, splashed up the square's puddles. We looked out of the corners of our eyes for fun: these two warrant officers hate each other.

'Now then, both together, Sergeant Majors: Royal Air Force —by the centre—quick—march. STOP STOP STOP!' Stiffy was dancing mad. The brass had followed the bandmaster, while the drums copied the S.M. A titter smudged its quick way across the five hundred strained faces of us airmen.

Stiffy went over to the band. 'Now then: band ready: one, two, three:'—everyone blared a cacophonous great note, haphazard. Stiffy beamed. 'That's it, Bandmaster.' 'Yes, Sir, that's the right way to do it,' agreed the bandmaster too emphatically, taking the wind for a moment from Stiffy's full body. 'Well, what was the other way, then?' he feebly rejoined ten paces too late.

We had been forgotten, nailed stiffly to attention, all this time the great ones experimented. A black east wind froze the sweat mushily over our skins. Some nerve in the flight seemed to have parted, leaving us useless. We could not slow-march or quick march or change direction. Even we muddled fours into two and twos into four on the march. Lofty downed me, in one wheel, by sliding on a banana skin. His great length fell across my track. I tried to jump him on the sudden but alighted with a bent ankle and flew headlong. 'Sergeant Jenkins,' roared Stiffy, red with rage, 'take those two idiots behind the wash-houses and fuck them.' 'Done it, Sir,' yelled Taffy, happy for a moment. But this was only momentary relief. As the hour passed conditions worsened. The Sergeant, ordinarily most patient and good-humoured all the day long, cursed and blistered, jabbed with his stick to hurt, booked real punishments. In vain. We were past amendment. This consoled me for hitherto I've been the only one dead-tired and ill after the P.T. which these fellows swore they loved:

but here and now it has got them all beat, though the instructor today was Hemmings to whom we pay only lip-service.

Yesterday Sergeant Cunninghame had taken us, with his science and pleasant keenness: for him we worked like Trojans. At the end we were puffed but happy. Some happiness: which in my case thinly survived the fit of sickness that overexercise brings on punctually in the tea-hour. This straining out every dreg of my dinner, twice or thrice a week, is a tiresome nuisance to me: though the effort to vomit silently in the latrine so that the others won't hear has given me an iron throat.

I proved this late in the night, dog-fighting. Dickson had arched me back over a bed and and was doing his utmost to throttle my windpipe. I got my chin forward in the Port Said manner and so my shortened muscles were able to hold out for minutes against the full squeeze of his fingers. Finally he drove a knee into the pit of my stomach, suddenly, and shifted his other hand to that fatal 'bollock-hold' of our impolite wrestling code. You bunch the things tightly and knead them. Not a brass monkey could resist such pain for sixty seconds.

I was yelling for pardon when Taffy's stick slid between us and pinked Dickson fairly in the tender spot under the armpit. He folded up beside me on the bed. 'What's the ruddy entertainment?' demanded Taffy, who'd come in to advise about tomorrow's ceremonial and allay the failure of today. 'I'm learning him,' invented Dickson on the spur of necessity. 'Yesterday, when we marched down-town on the bloody tram-lines, would he keep step? Would he fuck?' I was coughing and spitting too helplessly to deny the baseless yarn. 'Put that where the monkey put the nuts,' retorted Taffy. 'Now there's Gaby, the lovely blow-fly, my wet dream. Go and learn her: and let Ross alone. You want to grow a bit, sonny, before you take on Dickson.'

15

EXTRAS

We spend hours on semaphore, dotting ourselves on not-foggy days round all the edges of the valley to waft obscenities at one another with our arms. The fellows mis-spell these words phonetically, never having in their lives seen one of them in print. The Air Force, outside the Depot, doesn't use semaphore: so my brain remembers it no better than will carry me through the test at the end of the course. It's another kind of Euclid for the dullard recruits—a brain-food. Whereas lads brought up in the street cannot afford dullness.

School also is washed out after Depot. Squadrons have no compulsory education. So the zest of learning has gone out of that hour too. Not that it ever had a tremendous zest. I used to read *Faust*, which was pleasant: but the march there and the march back were burdensome straws to have piled on the back of our daily parades.

I'm sorry for the school-master, defeated after all by a physical circumstance. He stood so bravely in the other camp and avoided being an officer to us. Even he avoids being official, if he cannot miss that third rock of being a civilian—creatures from whom we feel strangely far, uplifted here by ourselves within our ring-fence. Every recruit feels always eyed, exposed, pedestalled: except at school, which we'd like to like, 169 for the master's friendliness: but there's that wearisome distance and the sense of waste it carries, like semaphore.

Wasted, too, I fancy are the hours devoted to teaching the man-handling of aircraft. Probationer-officers take us for that: and they do not put enough effort into it to meet our demand. We have almost a habit of trying hard, now. Some of us have read a little aerodynamics; so we expect the officers to know a great deal. Troops ask everything of their officers. Yet at the first lecture in the gloomy shed through which the wind blew damply upon the carcass of the imprisoned Bristol Fighter, Flying Officer Haynes confused incidence with the dihedral. Harder and I, standing there stockily like the rest, half lifted a secret eyelid one to the other. Drip, drip, drip, went Haynes' voice, wet as the wind.

It was worse later, on October the twenty-sixth, when another young officer deputised for Haynes. He tapped the epicyclic gear-case with his cane and airily told us, 'This is the Constantinesco gear. I won't muddle your heads explaining just how it works: but take it from me that it revs up the prop to twice the engine speed.' Our Allen, a country-bred, has been an air-gunner. I saw his legs wilt and his ears slowly redden with the news. He leaned forward crying, 'Eh': but my kick turned his mouth in time. It wouldn't be tactics to expose an officer before so new a crowd as ours: but it's a culpable carelessness. The R.A.F. claims to order our sitting and standing, our lying down and our going forth. *Soit:* but let its direction be supremely good. It is ourselves, our last gift, we give it.

Unfortunately Corporal Hardy saw me kick Allen and ran me for fooling on parade. He got me a smart sentence. 'Seen you before, haven't I?' said the flight commander. 'No defence? Then I'll make an example of you. You've had fair warning.' So I now pity myself nightly before and after an hour's jazz with full load on square: from which in a muck sweat I scramble into overalls and scrub some floor or other for the duty corporal (it's generally his sleeping bunk or daytime office) till he's pleased to let me go.

Not till ten o'clock do we defaulters finish for the night. That cuts short these notes but nothing will shorten my day, nor this self-pity which debilitates. I'd like to fight it off: but while my body has toughened here in the Depot and budded muscles in all sorts of unused places, my stoicism and silence of mouth gradually fade. I begin to blab to the fellows what I feel, just like any other chap.

16

OFFENSIVE

Trouble on the running track after dinner. We pay. An outside trainer had been brought in by the Commandant to train our flight for a walking relay-race of five laps: and Sergeant Cunninghame, the good little P.T. chief, had not known he was coming. They clashed and had a public row. It was referred to the officer in charge of physical training and Cunninghame lost. So after we had been walked nearly blind of both eyes he insisted on finishing our period of P.T., to vent his rage on us.

He doubled round and round the triangle, himself leading us at his sharpest pace: and he had not been walking laps. Then he dizzied us by volleys of starts, tumbling over immediate halts. This is like sawing at a brute's mouth. We were soon staggering, unable to heed his shrillest curses.

By tea-time the others were apparently recovered: but I was sick while I dressed for the sixth defaulters' drill, and sick again (tearingly on my empty stomach) when I came off it. Sergeant Walter had given us a horrible chasing, which made my next-rank man's nose bleed: but I seem to have grown callous to everybody's pains. Now it's ten at night and I'm too fagged to undress: the first night I sleep in my clothes, here. And in these overalls of all things. Cunninghame threatened, last thing, to crease us tomorrow. If he does that'll be my Waterloo, I think. Exactly five years since I felt as broke as this. I was a fool to try and be a man again.

Next day. Sergeant Cunninghame was absent: gone on week-end, they say: leaving Corporal Hemmings orders to do us in. Anyway Hemmings took us away from the gym to the thick grass behind the canteen and there kept us running and arms-and-legs-out-jumping, turning, and on the hands down for an hour and a quarter without break. Not one of his efforts tried to be a P.T. exercise: just 'mucking about,' inflicted maliciously in his meanest style. Only he does not know how to hurt a man. We responded in kind, swinging the lead so cunningly that the long spell took little out of us. In my own case I didn't even sweat much: whereas the regulation daily dose, conscientiously done, makes of me a most insanitary mess till my cold shower before bed.

Hemmings lost his temper as we laughed and leaped provocatively through the grass. The afternoon became a duel with him always attacking and us riposting by the pretence of enjoyment. No man could make fifty horses drink: so we won easily: and rubbed in our victory by swaggering over the parade-ground twenty minutes late for Stiffy's ceremonial. Stiffy had been ramping up and down (we are leading squad), sending messengers who vainly searched the gym for signs of us. Our corporal was nearly struck by lightning when we did appear; but he threw the blame in time on Corporal Hemmings, who was sent for at the double and blasted hip and thigh before everybody, for exceeding his duty. Stiffy couldn't know that he was trying to break us, by order.

Bad work, this scoring off. All the flights are talking of it tonight and the publicity compels our hut to go through with it, shirking and hitting back. It's the first parade we have shamefully scrounged but the circumstances of our wrong-doing make us cheerful sinners. Yet, none the less, it's an evil and competitive jubilation which may easily turn septic unless we are more moderate in victory than these fools of P.T. instructors who've thrown down the open gage.

Sailor was a little aerated this Friday night. He came in from the wet bar and summoned the huge Cook to court-martial for sodomy. 'He threw, Sir, a half-crown on the floor of the lavatory before a band-boy. The rest can be understood.' But Horder had not our late lamented China's suavity, as president of a court. So the fun languished.

Sailor did not. Suddenly he grappled Cook and with a wrestler's twist flung that thirteen stone of man across his shoulders. Cook turned there and strained upward, to ride his neck. Sailor tottered, caught the next bed behind his knees, and collapsed over it with his burden. Three, four, five others leaped upon them. From the human knot came his joyous cry of astonishment: 'Why, there's a fucker in the bed': and little Nobby's pathetic face, drowsy and sleep-puzzled, began to wriggle from under them. It reminded me of Sigurd under Fafnir's coils.

They disentangled. Sailor caught Nobby by the scruff with one strong hand, held him out, and with the other hand peeled off his pants and socks, cleanly, like a glove. The little yellow cock-robin legs frantically pedalled the air. Cook chuckled, snatched somebody's blacking-tin and with three swift passes of a boot-brush painted his doings jet-black. Torrents of applause. Exit Nobby, blaspheming, to the dark cold wash-house. The band struck up 'O God, our help in ages past.'

Enter Fane with tea and shortcake biscuit for Sailor, who took them, clapped biscuit over cup and inverted it successfully, crying, 'Elementary fucking science.' Cook sprang again on his back. Smash went the cup, splash the tea. They jazzed singing down the gangway, where Cook slid to the ground. A word, and Sailor bowed his head into his chest. Cook with a running leap was standing upright on his shoulders.

Sailor staggered forward. 'We are COMING,' he yelled— our dirty parody of a favourite ballad. Cook's crash to the floor was bone-shaking. 'We are arrived,' said he, in a breath-expelled whisper, across the instant of silence which followed on the crash. Our mandoline broke into the 'coming' song, and an unbuttoned ballet danced it stertorously, bellies in, bellies out. 'Star Evening News Standard,' howled Madden, the one-time paper boy. The hut was now properly alight.

I was on my back feeling as though I were growing into this bed which once had seemed hard. Tonight was my seventh and last punishment-drill and only in moments can I yet realise the ineffable freedom which will be tomorrow. Beside me Corton's flapping butter-churn of a voice rose to a screech, that his hour-long recital of a failed confidence-trick might continue to reach Horder across two beds and the din.

175

17

ANOTHER CHANCE

In the morning we went on dawn P.T., tightly girt as to the loins and ready, if anyone attacked us, to continue battle. The idiot Hemmings again got on to our mob: but the orderly officer who strolled over to see what the matter was sent him shortly back to his proper duty of supervision. Our round.

Afternoon P.T. was Corporal Small. We faced him shirkingly: but he stripped off his jersey to lead us himself and demonstrate the exercises. We saw his heart was engaged and not his spite. Therefore we played honestly back and forth the ill sequence. He kept us only forty minutes:—then said, 'Till last week we called you the posh flight. It won't be my fault if it isn't always. I take you, in future. Fall out now, and do your own work on the apparatus till time's up.'

A minute later the gym was like a Zoo, with airmen swinging on bars, swarming ropes, and crawling up the wrong sides of ladders, amidst cat-calls. I rested my sprained instep by traversing round the wall-girders on my wrists. Ten minutes to go. 'Show us that *grand circle*,' pleaded Sailor, to whom in the hut I'd tried to tell how this showy feat was compassed. Some demon of display took me. I jumped, suddenly confi-

dent, for the bar and at the second wild swing did it. The sky-
larking stopped abruptly. Because physical prowess is measur-
able with a rod, Englishmen exaggeratedly respect it. I find
myself higher in the general favour tonight.

18

AUDIENCE

Another monotonous failure of a church, in the grey cold rain which rusted our bayonets and made uncomfortable all our clothes. This apparatus of a parade service prejudices into blasphemy what thin chance organised worship ever had over vigorous men. Our blood distrusts and despises that something emasculate in the padre's ascetic face. He aims so crooked, too, when he tries to convict our party of sin. They are yet happy, being innocent of the reflection which creates a sense of sin.

Contact with natural man leads me to deplore the vanity in which we thinking people sub-infeudate ourselves. I watch, detachedly, my fingers twitching when I'm frightened, and smile and say 'Babinski'—judging myself now carried away by instinct, now ruling a course by reason, now deciding intuitively: always restlessly cataloguing each aspect of my unity. Like the foolish early Christians, with their Father, Son, and Holy Ghost, three sides of God, in that Creed for whose performance we just now had to stand up.

Hungry time has taken from me year by year more of the Creed's clauses till now only the first four words remain. Them I say defiantly, hoping that reason may be stung into new activity when it hears there's yet a part of me which escapes its rule: though it's as hard, by thinking, to take an inch off our complexity as to add an ell.

There it goes again: the conflict of mind and spirit. Whereas here are men so healthy that they don't chop up their meat into mince for easy digestion by the mind: and who are therefore intact as we are thereby diseased. Man, who was born as one, breaks into little prisms when he thinks: but if he passes through thought into despair, or comprehension, he again achieves some momentary onenesses with himself. And not only that. He can achieve a oneness of himself with his fellows: and of them with the stocks and stones of his universe: and of all the universes with the illusory everything (if he be positive) or with the illusory nothing (if he be nihilist) according as the digestive complexion of his soul be dark or fair. Saint and sinner touch—as great saints and great sinners.

After church they lectured us in the cinema on savings certificates, telling us we'd be glad of the money when we left the service and faced civil life. Why, we joined up because we'd failed in that civvy life! Don't remind us yet of that bad time with its money troubles. For seven years we are rid of it, able to afford the motor-bikes for which all our hut are keeping their shillings.

The lecturer was applauded and left the theatre: but we were still held in our seats. Finally Stiffy appeared, back-handing his moustache; and ascended the platform with a conscious smile. We clapped like hell. The self-consciousness deepened into a smirk which suggested, unfortunately, the anxious painted graces of a cheap professional. He advanced to the central chair and table, doing a little clown-business of astonishment at the cinema screen stretched above his head. We laughed and cheered.

Then he said that for long he had not had his monthly

179

grouse at us: and with a plunge into his matter he began
to denigrate women, as hindrances to man's bodily prowess.
'I want you fellows to swank, while you walk out.' (Plough-
ing the sand: the older the airman, the shyer he is of his fancy
dress. It's your recruit who flashes himself publickly.) 'Last
week, near Shepherd's Bush, I caught an airman, not from the
Depot, eating "land and sea" ' (fish and chips) 'off a barrow
in the street. That sort of sloppy creature's the most likely
target for bad women.' (Sensation in the back of the hall.
Bad women allure us in every novel: and we've read more
novels than we've met women.)

It was done genially, well done, and salted with rude items
of personal reminiscence which appealed to our vulgarity. It
all stank of vulgarity. We clapped and took every broad point
with that greasy laughter of the men's bar: a laughter which
held derision for the something craven that could so blatantly
appeal to our kindness.

He stooped further, to defend his square-folly of violence
and cursing, begging fellows not to be thin-skinned and resent
what was intended for their good. If it's policy, deliberate,
then he condemns himself dreadfully. We forbore with what
we believed an infirmity of temper. Now I saw his image falling
to our own level: though we may like him, familiarly, as one
of us, after this.

That's, of course, his place. Stiffy's an old army ranker,
product of wilder days than these, pre-war days when there
were ignorant classes. A pity. We'd have our officers not too
knowing—or at least not making clear their low knowledge:
officers so different that they'd not challenge our comparison
anywhere. Tall, vague, occasional beings, spendthrift and magnificent. Godlings to our groundlings.

19

ODD MAN OUT

Stiffy today took our flight for second morning period. It was a miracle of competence. His orders came in such perfect time that they were a pleasure to obey. He's more considerate as instructor than as parade-commander. We had an easy every fifteen minutes, and he was careful when repeating a practice to tell us just what improvement in our acts he wanted. Before he went we had forgiven him last week's lecture lapse. He's too supreme a drill-master for any man in uniform to despise.

For smartness we are now ranked first of the advanced squads: and we lead the show at cenotaph rehearsals. Sergeant Jenkins has worn well and the being under him has been all profit. When full of drink he may be sudden and dictatorial but we take no offence. Indeed, one day we were happy to help him. We were going on square when he muttered desperately to the leading files, 'For Christ's sake, look after yourselves. I'm that pissed I can't see where you are.'

It was true. He was reeling drunk: but we carried our drills off with so high a head that Stiffy never spotted the thing wrong. Taffy is an exemplar of the old disappearing fleshly and bloody N.C.O., the type which lasted from Smollett down to 1914, but which must disappear with the class from which it sprang. He's a master of arms' drill, and pleasedly content, therefore, with the masterpiece which is himself. It's a simple standard. On ceremonial parades Taffy emits a running fire of disrespectful comment, half under his breath, on Stiffy's every order and manœuvre. He often sorely tests our gravity.

In the hut we fellows remain good-tempered and solid, one with another: but we grow no personally nearer than on the third day. We attained an instant friendliness, and there stuck, three paces short of intimacy. To Kennington and others I make a joke of this depot life, and of myself, the slowest and silliest thing in it. 'Why don't you take a commission?' they ask, little knowing the feebleness of power. Airmen must help themselves. Good comes up from below. Yet when I face the Depot honestly, I know that I am dully miserable here.

First cause is the physical trouble—that my worn body has no margin against the exercises they prescribe for us: whence come aches and sprains, breathlessness, sickness, even that broken finger. I am dog-weary at the end of each week and begin every new week fatigued. Evening finds me tired-sick with the work done and fearful of the morrow: yet each free evening I snatch an hour in London, at the cost of as long in the train there and back. It's a craving for the feel of streets and to rub shoulders with an indifferent crowd: for no one sees a uniformed man. Their eyes note 'airman' or 'soldier,' registering class and not individual:—and they pass on. One is already a ghost while still full of blood and breath.

Dawn is a struggle to get up. I feel like Adam when the first trumpet of our daily resurrection goes. Night is a struggle to sleep, so in a crowd. If I might be alone a moment: yet it's now too cold for out of doors or wet: and we dare not dull the boots whose polish will be looked for first thing in the morning. The hut is too populous and chattery: homelike, for its sort: but I'm a strange sloth strayed into this section. My hope of getting back to human-kind by fettering myself to my likes, seems to have hopelessly failed. I'm odder, here, than when by myself in Barton Street: the oddness must be bone deep.

At Oxford I was odd, too: my only familiar man the whisky-lover, who after a day and a night locked into his room would invade me at dawn conjuring me, by all that was friendly between us, to find him a way out of life: some way which would save the insurance money for his people. In officers' messes too, I've lived about as merrily as the last-hooked fish choking out its life in a boat-load of trippers.

In those days I used to radiate discomfort to the surrounders: while here it is only my single person which will not fit. The fellows take my digestibility for granted: indeed, they are astonishingly good to me. Every tub, in the services, must stand on its own bottom: but I have privileges, am deferred to. Since China left, they have even come to leave me untouched. China would maul and handle me till I longed to scream.

Yet the basis of this dull misery I feel is not just physical. Weariness I have often fought down and conquered with endurance, my spare quality, which I have in such abundance that it fails to be a virtue. The root-trouble is fear: fear of failing, fear of breaking down. Of course my vanity will suffer, if I prove worse than the others in their work. Also I seem stiff and clumsy of body. That hurts me: this miserable flesh should do my service without complaint. I don't want to be laughed at, or to have reason to laugh at myself; and also there is the school-fear over me, that working against hazardously-suspended penalty which made my life from eight to eighteen miserable, and Oxford, after it, so noble a freedom.

Here we will be (we are) punished for any mistake, for any falling short of standard; or of requirement, or fancied requirement: or punished merely because someone thinks it's about time we were. Headquarters sent our flight commander the reminder one day, 'Mr. Maclaren, there is not enough crime in your flight.' I've been lucky to get off all but three charges: and to that last one I did not wish to make any defence: but I have seen others suffer glaring injustice, just to satisfy the system. So I go in terror, not of the punishment (man suffers only so far, and then pain fades), but of the state of being punished, the notoriety or pity of it. That week when I was catching it badly the fellows vied to do me little kindnesses, showing they were sorry for me. It was like hot fingers stroking my shame.

20

IN THE GUARD-ROOM

At dinner-time Headquarters suddenly informed Sergeant Jenkins that he was next for guard, with every man below five feet eight in his flight. The tall men are for memorial service tomorrow. The figure gives a large surplus of shorties: however, Taffy's chosen his guard-party, and I am one.

He was angry about it. We've been so concentrated on ceremonial and cenotaph for weeks that our routine training has ceased. P.T., ceremonial, school, P.T., ceremonial:—that's been our round, day after day. Guard-duties are a specialty and we've not even touched them. Taffy went to tell Stiffy this, and said we couldn't do a guard. 'Nonsense,' replied Stiffy. 'It'll be Harry Tate of course: but I don't care for once.' 'All right,' said Taffy, 'orders is orders. Only don't call me responsible.' Behind the hut he gave us a first idea of guard-mounting; so we scrambled through the faintly silly preliminaries not too ill.

I was cast for first sentry. Along came Sergeant Major II, the decent one. On his passing me I ported arms. He gave me a look, hesitated and went on. He came back through the gate. I ported again. 'Why?' he asked simply. 'Must do something, Sir, for a Sergeant Major, I suppose.' He laughed. 'Oh, you're the rag guard. Only don't do it to anyone else.'

The evening fatigue swung past, overalled, in fours. I upped my rifle to the present. Sergeant Poulton glared at me. 'What the hell do you mean, sentry, presenting to a fatigue party?' 'Token of respect, Sergeant: they do all the work.' Taffy's laugh rippled out behind me, from the shadow of the verandah. 'You piss off, Pissquick. Nobody loves you, in my squad.'

It was the night of the sergeants' mess dance. Taffy, dripping obscenities, sat on the doorstep and checked the guest-women coming in: over fifty of them. He had for each a salutation which brought giggles, a blush or a squawking laugh. In his day Taffy was a 'lad': now he prefers beer to fornication. I noticed he did not use his own manner to one single woman. Do they ever hear men's real voices? Till two in the morning sergeants, more or less unsteady, rolled in and out of the gates. Only eight of the fifty women had gone out of the legitimate exit by dawn.

A bucket of drink was carried to the guard-room as Taffy's share of the dance's refreshment. Jock Mackay, too tight to dance, came over to help Taff drink it. The two warriors sat beside the stove, ignoring us, to chop tales of old wild service, of campaigns in India and France, of adventures in mean streets: dipping, between tales, their enamelled mugs into the beer-bucket and hiccoughing it down.

After rounds at four in the morning they sang for thirty minutes the marching songs (airs official, words the troops' own) of all the regiments they'd met. That finished, they stood up to drill. A moment before they had been swaying drunk. The touch of arms sobered them: they went through the manual from A to Z before us perfectly. More than mechanically perfect it was: a living, intelligent pattern and poem of movement. Auld Lang Syne . . . and Jock staggered homeward to sleep it off. Taffy fell down on our sleeping bench and was off in a moment.

Dawn came or half-came. Reveille, and the trumpeter sounded in the road by headquarters. Dimly I remembered the guard had a reveille performance. 'Sergeant,' I called, urgently shaking Taffy's shoulder. He jerked up before the call had ended, and in a moment realised the situation and our lateness. In two strides he was at the door, out of it, on the murky verandah. 'Guard attention: advance arms' . . . the whole procedure of morning salute he shouted into the blank mist, lest the orderly officer be on the prowl listening for us.

We guards were meanwhile struggling back from sleep off the benches, rubbing eyes and settling the night-tossed equipment into place on our shoulders. 'What's old Taffy's row all about?' wondered Park. The Sergeant stepped back to the door, mustered us with a glance of his laughter-inflamed eye and gave a last yell: 'Guard, to the guard-room, DISMISS!' 'A bloody smart lot,' he grumbled, at us cackling over his presence of mind. Out came the threatening stick and we shoved our fists into our mouths to be sober. Highly irregular, Taffy's whacking us: but we love him even for that. He's a pleasure to serve. We mollified him with the drainings of the beer-bucket. 'Good lad,' he said to me, at length.

It had fallen to little Nobby, sentry at the solitary laundry gate, to call Stiffy's batman at half-five, that the great man's cup of tea might be ready for him before work. Nobby crept timorously into the eerie black house, through the kitchen door, and incontinently lost his way. He opened one door—a box-room: another, and there was the obscure outline of a bed. He felt over it with his hands, to put them straight upon

187

a warm face. 'Coo,' he cried, jumping back. A head, two heads, rustled up from the pillows. 'Is that Stiffy's batman?' queried Nobby, shaking: and the great known voice wrathfully clanged back, 'No, it's Stiffy.'

21

STIFFY

Every camp needs its dominant: and ours has drawn the lot of Stiffy, who is very masterful. He does not pretend to be an officer: perhaps he harbours a latent grudge against the officer-class: he so likes to take them down before us. 'Mr. Squire, your damned cap isn't fit for parade.' Indeed, he wants to be the sole ruler here and humiliates the sergeant major, the sergeants, even the corporals, by public curses.

Having thus got rid of competition Stiffy turns to build up. He tries to impose on us his standard which is the barrack-square, pure and simple. To fail there is Failure: and things not done on square do not seriously exist. With our lips we follow him: but our acts are not in accord. We all know Sailor to be the best man of us. Yet on square he is nothing. We set him over us, voluntarily, because of his forcefulness. My influence is wide, off-duty. Yet I'm painfully, consciously, awkward at drill.

Even Stiffy is not consistent. He subordinates all our life to drill-periods and then blacks drill by calling it a means to make us airmen. Lip-service, that. Stiffy has not an idea what an airman is, while he has an idea—more, a conviction—that drill is worth doing perfectly for its own sake. The queer regard of a grown man for bodily antics!

189

If Stiffy's staff all believed with him, they might carry us along: we have the attitude of being taught. But the corporals assure us it's army bull-shit which does not persist beyond this depot. By their inadequacy the Depot fails to be continually fierce. It is disjected, a place of fits and starts, full of new-nesses which are uncertainties. Particularly the school (not under Stiffy), where they beg us to be intelligent and to work for our private sakes. So school opposes square.

But failingly. We grow sheepish. Classes with teachers go well: private-study men languish or nod over their books. My French class showed me the fatuity of beginning to learn a book subject, while our bodies were in the mill. We have grown to do only what we're told. In the first eagerness we did more and suffered for the crime of initiative. We were eager for hot baths, to wash all over. Now, being almost troops, we know that our inspected part is from the hair on the neck to the top edge of the gym vest. It takes little cleaning: so we learn con-servation of energy, which alone enables us against the rush of work.

This learning to be sterile, to bring forth nothing of our own, has been the greater half of our training and the more painful half. Obedience, the active quality, is easy. We came in want-ing to be very obedient and we are pathetically grateful to Taffy for ordering us about from dawn till dark. The common tone and habit of the camp helped us and taught us obedience, atmospherically.

It's quite another thing to learn to flop, passively, when the last order's completed: hard to wait supinely for the next. Fel-lows want to forestall orders out of self-respect. Self-respect is one of the things troops have to jettison, as a tacit rebellious-ness of spirit, a subjective standard. We must have no standards of our own. Our decency is in the care of the officers and

190

N.C.O.s, when they remember it; and our honour is what they think good enough for us. After a while of this regime troops' intellects and wills go back to God, who made them. It's queer to see our minds bend when we lean on them. As walking sticks to stay instinct or character over a rough place they are now as useless as a stem of ivy.

Our hut used to arrive at an opinion by discussion, by contradicting the early word that the first fool rushed out. Later this turned into instinct. We have come, unknowing, to a corporate life. Today we think, decide, act on parade without a word said. Men are becoming troops when like one body they are sluggish (to a bad instructor) mulish (when angered) willing (to an open-hearted man). We have attained a flight-entity which is outside our individualities. The self-reliance each has singly lost is not lost to us all. As a flight we're stiff-necked and spirited as though the excellencies of Sailor and Snaggle had been buttered thinly over all the fifty heads. The person has died that to the company might be born a soul. For six weeks more: then we are trained men and our unity will be broken into fifty bits and scattered. But we are no nearer knowing, today, whether the new fifty will be their ancient selves, or microcosms of the flight, than we were on that first day when we came in so shyly through the gate with Sergeant Sheepshanks.

22

GAOL-DELIVERY

A fellow came running to me from the orderly-room: a letter was just through from Air Ministry, posting me instantly to a unit. So I dodge the last weeks of depot training and the orgy of fitness-tests with which it closes. The Lord be praised. Someone, Trenchard probably, has been looking after me. Incidentally we heard much more of Trenchard that time we were on guard. The corporal of the night had been his batman: the one who went out with him to Egypt in our boat last year. Of course, he did not know me: but all right, whenever Taffy wasn't talking, we egged out of him yarns about his master. The eyes in which it is good to be a hero are one's valet's.

By tea-time news had reached the Office. Corporal Hardy came back and warned me for orderly-room tomorrow at nine o'clock. 'Old Stiffy's hopping mad at a man being sent off before the end of training. Chewed my fucking balls up, something cruel.' So I went there knocking at the knees and gave Stiffy a wonderful salute, in palliation. He looked down at me as if I were ugly and ill-smelling:

'How long you here?'

I told him.

'How much drill d'you know?'

'Very little, Sir.'

'How's that?'

'First month's all fatigues, Sir: since, it's been all cenotaph practice.'

He heard me in a silence of disgust.

At nine-forty last night, so soon as rounds were over, the east end of the hut, Fane, Park, Corton, Garner, Madden and company threw their cleanest bed-sheet over the table, put a form each side and spread the top with food from the Y.M. and the canteen. There were Zepps in a cloud (sausages and mashed) and Adam and Eve on a raft (Hoxtonian for fried eggs on toast) as main dishes: with every available trimming of cheese, tomatoes, and wads, penny or tuppenny. Three water-bottles of 'Stall tea were the finishing touches of this feast for which they'd put up every last copper of their joint pay. It was their farewell to me, who surely must have been a little human here: no one ever ventured to banquet me, before.

These distinctions of an east and a west end to our hut arose naturally when we first settled in it. Pound-note speakers, men who were book-learned and of posh trades, collected round the western stove: and those who swore by the pure Camberwell gravitated towards the other. In the centre slept the neutrals. Time absurdly made me almost the unconscious arbiter of the west end. Westerners would bait the east end, gently, as a bit of the real life-with-knobs-on.

Tongues often joined battle of a Saturday night. The east liked its beer: liked more than it could carry. Particularly Corton. He was a burly fellow, who'd end his arguments with the invitation to put 'em up. No one in the hut, bar Sailor and perhaps Dickson or Cook, could have matched him. Corton was not one of my first admirations: when in drink (and each seventh day he was nasty drunk) a little streak of what seemed gross used to declare itself in him.

He'd charge the door open, and roll in from the latrine all uncleaned, with his dropped breeches flouncing round his knees. He'd throw down the blankets of the first empty bed and squat there with a leer on his mouth, rocking and rubbing his nakedness on the sheets. When this had cooled him enough, he'd slide his heavy body by his hands over the bed-end, to stand crowing and pointing with happy finger. 'Oh, shitty,' he'd say, 'he's shit the bed.' Afterwards, to piss, he'd creep from pretended sleeper to sleeper watering in each pair of cleaned boots till he could squeeze out no more.

My squeamishness over him kept itself secret for fear of seeming high-brow: also it knew that its body could not fight Corton's. Others, however, began to moan behind his back. Perhaps Sailor said something to him: anyway after the third week-end the bad habit ceased. During that month the west had lost some airs and the east had learned some: while we all in the daily commerce of misery had found what realities lay behind the airs.

Fortunately for me: for when I fell out with the Corporal over that refused loan, a week before my last jankers, he shifted Corton up the hut to be my oppo. The intended spite missed fire. Upon near acquaintance the big man proved rarely, bluntly, honest. Quite near acquaintance: we were three feet apart all night. Nor did he ever hurt me, when he was in drink. He'd bend over my pillow, gently stroking my hair and murmuring, 'Naughty, naughty,' while the hut, looking for me to be flung out suddenly, shivered in delight.

At the melancholy end of the feast, over the ruined food, the givers began to say things about losing me: evoking goodbyes which stung terribly in my throat. To my collected mind this posting is a godsend: yet soon, now in fact, I'll start regretting it. Anonymity is a yearly-rarer dish for me. Only by hiding that past identity can I get squarely treated, like the plain run of men: and then I discover myself as rather less useful a person that the average of my kind. A sound lesson in modesty: but a costly lesson, for acting the new man demands a day-and-night vigilance which only physical excitement can brace me to keep up.

Here I have been on my own, and up against it: stretched almost beyond my failing body's bearing to sustain the competition of youth. Depot will have the backward-looking warmth of probably my last trial: survived at least, if not very creditably. Though sometimes I've laughed aloud while I cried hardest into my note-book. And the gain of it is that I shall never be afraid of men, again.

For I have learned solidarity with them here. Not that we are very like, or will be. I joined in high hope of sharing their tastes and manners and life: but my nature persists in seeing all things in the mirror of itself, and not with a direct eye. So I shall never be quite happy, with the happiness of these fellows who find their nectar of life, and its elixir, in the deep stirring of some seminal gland. It seems I can get nearest it by proxy, by using my powers (so sharpened by experience and success in war and diplomacy) to help them preserve their native happiness against the Commandants and Poultons of this world.

The R.A.F. for me is now myself: a vocation absolute and inevitable beyond any question under the sky: and so marvellous that I grow hot to make it perfect. I have hated to see the bloom of its virginal recruits wasted by the inept handling here. My own injuries are risible always: every man's own injuries are risible always, only too easy for him to forgive, if, indeed, they ever earn that great word 'forgive.' Could a Poulton, however early he got up in the morning, collect enough subtlety to hurt me memorably? But when he offends the others I am indignant. He sins against the Air.

PART THREE

Nearly three years pass

AN EXPLANATION

I had the ambition—before I turned back in 1923 and saw the inadequacy of my Seven Pillars in the cold light of revision—to write a real book: and I thought to find its subject in the Royal Air Force.

The foregoing chapters were noted down night by night in bed at the Depot, as foundations for the intended book: not exactly word for word:—in their natural state sentence was twisted over sentence like the entrails in a man's belly; and here I've pulled them out into one string, like a pound of sausages:—but essentially these are my depot notes.

Depot would have been a porch, a short porch of selected scenes, to the book I meant to write for the incomparable Hogarth upon Life in a Flying Flight, which is the veritable air force: but my sudden dismissal from Farnborough knocked that experience on the head. When, three years too late, I was allowed back to what has since been my element and fellowship, things could not be the same as they had been in 1922.

Therefore I've arranged for you (Hogarth is gone, so you must be Edward Garnett, to whose sense of form I owe so much) every single sentence of my Depot notes. Not a recorded word is missing, nor a word added, yet. But I cannot leave the tale at this point. The Depot I knew was a savage place. That is now changed: so for fairness' sake I've picked out the few following extracts, mainly from letters to my friends: in the hope that they may give an idea of how different, how humane, life in Cadet College was. There is no continuity in these last pages—and a painful inadequacy: but perhaps some glint of our contentment may shine from between my phrases into your eyes.

How can any man describe his happiness?

1

RAIL JOURNEY

Being dressed for my train-journey was like a dose of jankers: tunic, breeches and puttees:—that's a hot kit. Marching boots so hobbed that every pavement became a skating rink. My overcoat (mid-August). Complete equipment so thickly clayed that at any movement its brown powder rained like pollen on my clothes and neighbours. Full pack, weighing many pounds. A bayonet—for the Great Northern Railway, ye gods! Looped over the bayonet, a little haversack of cold beef and bread, balanced on the right side by a filled water-bottle. This poor man's camel had dumbly accepted its load so far: but at the two-and-a-half pounds of lukewarm water it found voice. Regulations. You're in the Depot still. Hold your blasted tongue or you'll go inside the guard-room.

At the station gate they threw on my shoulder (knocking my cap off) the kit-bag of all my spare goods: only eighty more pounds. For the 'stiffy airman' a porter would be a crime as capital as an umbrella. Before I reached the end of the platform, sweat was running like a hot bath down my arms and legs.

The trip slowly convinced me that this military equipment was not designed for peace-time trains. I had become too wide to advance frontally through any carriage door. In each queue or press I jabbed the next man with a buckle in the mouth, or browned the next woman with my equipment's clay. When I sat, the little side-bags and skirts of my clobber occupied two places. The pack fouled the back of the seat, so I had to perch all the while on the edge, and block the gangway.

The old lady next me in the underground wore a flippant skirt, all doo-dahs. My scabbard chape enlarged one of these. She rose up and went, more fretted even than the skirt. I bulged with relief into her extra space: but my water-bottle tilted nose-down on the arm rest, and filled the vacant seat with a secret lake. Then, fortunately, I changed trains.

It was all changing trains: and as I learnt how, I stood in the vestibule for the short trips, to lessen my unavoidable nuisance to the public: and took off my harness and overcoat for the long spells. That was much better, until water began to drip from the rack. So I disentangled the silly bottle from its straps, and emptied it out of the window (into the window next door, as we soon heard).

By Victoria I was fed up with changing trains, and funked the press of lunch-hour in the city. So I climbed into an empty bus for King's Cross, taking the seat nearest the door. The top, of course, was out of my power. We were past Russell Square and again empty, when the conductor came back, and looking down on my cap's polished peak said, 'Ah, we didn't wear our marching order nicely blancoed in them days. You wouldn't think it, but I was one of the original four thousand in your mob. That was in '14; days of the war. Bit before your time, sonny.' 'Yes, dad,' I murmured, blandly.

At King's Cross a half-hour to wait: good, for the trains today were crowded. I got a corner and sat down. The scurrying crowds peered in and passed: people do not travel with service fellows if they can help it. We had a quiet long run all across the sunny fens. Another change was due at tea-time. I got up to resume my harness, for railway platforms abound with service police, who report airmen not wearing it properly.

To put on equipment in camp you hold it out in front, dart one arm suddenly through it and with a cast of the disengaged arm and a lively whirl of the body on the left foot, spin into the rest. This calls for eighty square feet of floor space. To attempt it in a crowded compartment would be to knock too many teeth out. For a while I tangled myself like a fly in a web, trying to slide into it quietly: but then a grown man in the carriage rose and held it for me silently and professionally, like a strait waistcoat. A minor effect of the war's military education of England had been notably to ease the lot of an airman travelling by rail.

Another change, another journey, dusk, detrainment, and a long road. The lights of the camp were like a town, east and west of the arrow-straight tarmac. Time I got serious. Positively that was a guard-room ahead. We feel these buildings by some instinct. My curiosity grew very keen. Here I would spend years: what was its first impression? Distinctly good. The sentry had only a cane, no belt or rifle. Inside, the dazzle of light showed me a mob of service police. Will have to look out for them. Their sergeant took my papers, and directed me to 83 hut, down the second path on the left. 83 hut, it seemed, was kept furnished with beds for chance arrivals. That sounds like consideration for the men. I peered into its not very bright corners, and guessed it empty: but someone in the bunk heard the scrape of my boots, for its door opened. Out came a solitary man: an A/C like myself.

'Hullo, where'd you spring from? Depot? Well, you're in luck here: this place is cushy. Any bed you like: there's no one but us two. I'm sort of hut orderly. Spot of grub in the canteen? Right O. . . . Roll-call? Yes, they do have a sort of a one, I fancy, down in the lines: but the corp won't tool all the way up here. Your next stop'll be Adjutant tomorrow. I'll tool you along.' He was the runner at headquarters.

'What about a wash?' I asked, beginning to peel off the loathly clothes, all gummed to me by the hot trip. Barnard waved to the hut's entrance, through a shallow annexe. 'Help yerself: two baths, hot and cold.' After Depot it seemed too good: but it was true.

2

B FLIGHT

I woke up feeling easy. I shall like this place. Today is glorious with sunlight. The runner and I ate a slow breakfast, of service type, and I helped him sweep out the few rooms and passages of headquarters by half-past seven before the first officers showed up. I waited on till just after eleven, when they had leisure for me.

'I've seen you before,' said the first adjutant. 'Were you at Depot three years ago?' I admitted it, in a tone which checked his asking more. 'You'll go to B Flight. Just book his particulars, Sergeant Major, and send him down.'

I spent the afternoon shifting kit into Hut 105, and in drawing bedding. There's a corporal in charge of the hut and its dozen fellows. The flight is only fourteen A/Cs, him, and a sergeant: and we all live together in this neat little hut of sixteen beds. It's holidays just now. Holidays sound queer to me: but it seems our reason of existence here is to maintain the machines on which the cadets learn flying, and in August the College shuts down. Most of the irks take their month's leave then. The others do odd fatigues to fill in the empty days.

3

MANNERS

Up ever so early, but with this wonderful sunshine filling the hut from soon after five, it feels sticky lying abed. The place is country. I wandered across to the reception hut, where I'd spent the first night, and helped myself to a hot bath, quietly, not to wake Barnard. That had been his stipulation, in making me free of his water. The reason he's so favoured with it is that Hut 83 backs on the cadets' lines, and they must have hot water always. I thank them. So shall I.

Back, and everybody yet asleep. I made my bed up, Depot fashion, and went to breakfast. When I came in again, my neighbour was regarding the bed with disfavour. 'You bobbing, mate?' he queried. 'This here's not the fuckin' Depot, you know.' Out came the Corporal from the bunk. 'Where do you come from, anyhow?' 'Depot, Corporal,' I rejoined, bringing my heels together as I'd been taught. 'Well, just you forget it, see? And put your bed like this.' With three or four deft twists of the hand my bedding sprawled and poke'd its corners to the four airts, like a dissipated haycock. 'And you don't stand to attention in the Air Force when you talk to an N.C.O.'

'Right O, Corporal,' I laughed, daring a pounce at this new easy manner. In Depot 'Right O' to a strange corporal would have put me on a charge. The Corporal rounded on me like a trodden snake. 'And cut that right out, too, you and your "Corporal." Want to make a bloody cunt of me? My name's Geordie: get it? This is Cadet College. Wash out all that blarsted bull-shit you've bin taught. You're in the Air Force now. Fucking corporals in the Depot are bigger 'n wing commanders outside.'

He's right: it isn't the Depot. That assertion of manner has passed, with its boastful carriage, the abrupt heely stride, the clatter of boot-nails. These fellows can saunter as if no eye was on them: and when they want to hurry they nip along, quiet-footed, with a spring in it. Perhaps they're allowed rubbers on their soles. Their uniforms, too, seem *worn:* not so much badges of service, as the private clothing of their profession. Blue is a reducing agent. The modest colour and spare fit prompt its wearers to seem a handy size.

4

A FIRST NOTE

I'm just going over to the hangar to continue valeting aeroplanes. We do it lazily, killing time for the new term to open and our cadets to come. They say we 'sweat like buggery' in term time. This life pleases me all over: the people not so much: but I'm a slow starter, always unfavourably impressed, whenever I'm dropped into a hut-full of strangers. It is only after their crudities have been well learned and forgiven that the more interesting core appears. Their limited expression hides them at first: the monotony of their adjectives revolts me. Not so bad, pretty good, fucking good:—there are positive, comparative, superlative, for everything. Nothing's funny, or vivid, or familiar unless it travesties our sexuality. However, give them time. Some people get on terms directly: but in return give a great deal of themselves away, as fast.

5

LODGINGS

I wonder how you would like our nights? The hut is so small for the sixteen of us: a row of beds down each long wall, a table and two forms in the narrow middle, a square stove. In the centre of each short wall, a door: one gives on the open air, one to a wash-house-shower-bath-lavatory annexe, which makes a porch to the eastern or wintry side of the hut.

We, as I said, are sixteen: fourteen men, a corporal, and a sergeant. Our beds are of iron sheeting, and slide in. Very hard they feel, for the first nights. The mattresses are three little square brown canvas cushions, rammed solid with coir. Biscuits they call them.

The next bed is only an arm's reach from mine. It is odd to have the other man's whispering breath so near my pillow all the night. His name is also Ross: a Scotchman from Devonshire, just married, a nice fellow: which is good fortune since a rough bedfellow is exhausting. Riches wholly deliver a man from bedfellows:—a privilege, and a loss, too: for the intimate jostling of like and like is often as fertile as it's disconcerting.

Airmen sleep very restlessly, always. Partly it may be due to the hard beds, on which a man cannot turn without a groan and half-waking up to lift the hip: yet turning is needful because the hardness cramps our bodies, if we do not constantly shift them.

So the night to one who, like me, lies much awake is never fully quiet. There are groans and mutterings, and dream-words. They all dream, always: and sometimes they say beastlike things in their sleep.

I wonder how far I betray myself in the first part of the night, which is my sleeping time? In the Army, when on armoured car work I was being driven unskilfully by other fellows all day, my nervousness so increased that it turned to fever and delirium, and I talked like a river half one night. None of them would ever tell me what I said: but in the morning they looked at me strangely.

Our nights are white. The ten windows have been catching the moonlight, since I came, and the walls are lime washed a water colour: so that even starlight and the reflections of the distant lamps over there in the College make them gleam. It seems never dark, here in the north, for very soon after I wake up there comes the first touch of dawn. I feel like a fish in a still cistern, dreaming away these short hours. The sleep in my eyes is like water to dull them and the quietness is real, compared with the noise of day. If you could hear the iron hangar throbbing at this moment, with the running up of a 260 h.p. Rolls-Royce engine at nineteen hundred revs!

Yet the quiet does not last long. Its beginning is delayed by the late men not coming in till midnight or after: and they may come in stumbling, unsteadily knocking puttee-defended legs against bed-foot after bed-foot, swearing or chuckling inanely, the while. And the end of quiet is at reveille.

The reveille here is the most grateful of any camp I know. There are no whistles or bugle calls (how every serving soldier hates a bugle) and no orderly sergeant to bray hideously. Just we let the dawn rouse us. As the five tall windows each side the whitewashed hut brighten, the sleepers stir, more and more frequently, till they are completely awake. At this season that is yet too early to rise: for we have no unavoidable duty before breakfast, between half-past seven and eight. So the crowd lie dozing, or sleeping; or read or chat lowly to one another. This quiet prelude to the working day was the first and greatest beatitude of College.

I get up soonest of all, and nip over in the running vest and shorts which are my sleeping suit, to 83 hut, of the opposite lines, across a grass meadow. There I bath. Such a funny little bath, a square brown earthenware socket, like a drain, in the cement floor. Fortunately I'm little, too, and if I tuck up like a tailor I can just squat in it, as if I were a dirty dish in a sink, with six inches of warm water round me: and there I splash, and shave, and splash again. This is heaven on a cold morning: and Cadet College faces the North Sea and can be colder than any spot in England. Indeed we are particular to score the low temperature record every winter.

About seven I run back to the hut and enter noisily, for a signal to the others, who begin to exhort one another to get up. We make our beds, heaping the three biscuits in a column and wrapping four blankets in a fifth, with an intervening sandwich of sheets. Then boot-cleaning, button-polishing, sweeping out the bed-area and doing my weekly one of the fourteen jobs into which hut-maintenance is divided. If it's stove-black-leading, another wash. Then I grab knife, fork and mug and run over to the mess-deck for breakfast.

6

BODY AND SOUL

The mess-deck is long and bare, chill as a vault, and moist-smelling from its rows of white-scrubbed heavy tables and forms. On each table is a pile of twelve plates. As we come in we put our mugs on the end of a table. When he has counted twelve waiting mugs, the supervising corporal throws down a tin ticket: and the end men, the last comers, go to a serving hatch and draw their bucket of tea and an iron ration tin, holding twelve breakfasts.

The food in this camp is miserable: little and bad. Hence the flourishing canteen. Today's offer to our appetites was a scrap of cold ham, swimming for its desperate life in a flood of tinned tomato juice. Yesterday it was steak, stewed to a good imitation string. The irks grumble also at the tea, because it is not strong, and not sweet. I am thankful for both lacks: and wish, besides, that it was not hot. A pity that men strive to surpass water, that cheap, easy, affectionate and subtle drink.

A feature of Cadet College is that we have not to wash our plates. It is done for us (not well, but who looks a mercy in the mouth?) by a special squad whose utter greasiness of life and work is redeemed by unlimited pickings in food. All that we leave is theirs. So every belly-favouring man jumps at the job. I ran the risk of being put among them, when I enlisted as unskilled: but after my sorrows in Farnborough in 1923 I dared not try for photographer again. For the time, though, the risk of mess-orderly is past, with my enrolment in B Flight.

After breakfast we go on parade: about two hundred of us men, and one hundred cadets, would-be officers. We form three sides of a hollow square. On the eastern, open face is a flagstaff. We face this, after some shifting back and forward. The R.A.F. colours are broken at the peak: the trumpeter (imported for the ceremony from East Camp) blows a royal salute: the cadets, who have rifles, present arms. We who have nothing, stand still.

The salute is the shrillest note a trumpet can sustain. It goes through us, however densely we close our pores. The thrill of exceeding sharpness conquers, in blades, sounds, tastes. Everything else upon the square, a huge asphalt place, hut-circled and echoing, is deadly still. Imagine a raw wind, and a wet early sunshine, making our shadows on the tarred ground the exact blue colour of our clothing.

After the salute Jews and Roman Catholics fall out: while the chaplain says prayers: we all bowing our heads meekly, standing at ease. Having been prayed over (a little ironical, it sounds, the petition that this day we fall into no sin, neither run into any kind of danger, when some of us will fly an hour later, and all of us have been misdoing and swearing obscenely since the dawn: however . . .), at last the Wing Commander dismisses us: and we march off by flights to the hangars and our day's work.

7

THE HANGAR

'The hangar and our day's work.' That sounds an easy picture to draw. Now, for a year and more, it has been the staple of my life: but not yet can I see its truth in sober prose, though always I am thinking of it, always trying to see it.

The facts of course are there. Our hangar is a girder frame, sheathed in iron. The floor is of concrete, without one pillar or obstruction across its main expanse. The mere space of it is rewarding, to a daily dweller in low rooms. Too rewarding, perhaps. An airman alone in it feels puny and apprehensive. It is as great as most cathedrals, and echoes like all of them put together. We have parked fourteen aeroplanes within its central hall.

The southern face is wholly door: giant twenty-five-foot leaves of iron, hanging on wheels from their top edge, and rolling back, leaf by leaf, with the roll of thunder when three or four of us put our shoulders to the work. Then, on every fine day, the sun streams in, gilds our kites, and plants fifty-yard ladders of dancing motes in the dingiest corners of the huge place. Also the sun evokes the private smell of B hangar: something in which oil and acetone and hot metal have part.

I like the hangar well in storms. The darkness and its size conspire to make it formidable, ominous. The leaves of the closed doors tremble in the guides, and clap boomingly against the iron rails. Through their crevices, and the hundreds of other crevices, packs of wind hurtle, screaming on every high note of the scale, to raise devil-dances across the dusty floor. Screech, boom: and the rain after the squall is like all the rifle-fire of an army. That shivering moment Tim will choose to issue from the office, and set all our hands to sweep the half-acre of concrete.

At night it looks a palace. We switch on lamp after lamp, high in the roof, and a wedge of golden light pours through the open front across the illimitable aerodrome which runs up, saucer-like, to a horizon like the sea, and sea-coloured, of waving grey-green grass. In this stream of light puny figures, eight or ten of them, swim, at a game of push and pull around the glitter-winged Bristol Fighters or Nine Acks. They drag them one by one into the lighted cave: then the doors clang shut, the lights go out: and the dwarfs trickle out from a dwarf-door in rear, across grass and gravel, bedwards.

Tim is the Flight Commander. He's a jewel. We enjoy every massive inch of him. It's a sight to see him shaking with silent mirth when somebody is foolish. We can watch the smile coming, from behind him, by the slow widening of his jowl. It's another sight to see us scuttling with fright behind busses and round corners, when word goes forth that Tim has a weed on. Tim is our barometer; he sets the flight's weather. B Flight has the most exciting climate in the world.

At Cadet College the R.A.F. officer comes back to his own, in the foreground of authority, with the flight commander as the absolute fore-head. Our fifteen-man flight has three or four officers. Can they help meeting us, speaking to us, knowing us? We are the hands who actually push their machines about: on

215

our vigilance and duty the officers' lives depend, for hours every flying day.

Because officers take their proper places, sergeants and corporals take theirs. Gone is the Prussian N-c-ocracy of Depot. They become our representatives, not chosen by us perhaps, but nominated from our best with tacit approval. We accept them as useful creatures who intervene and parley for us with the government. If they do not function to our bidding, we can go behind their backs, informally, any day out on the drome where we have the officers to ourselves. The incumbent give-and-take makes us a family: a happy family if the grown-ups are good, an unhappy family when they do not pull together. Praise be to Tim that B Flight can never suspect a meanness in its constitutional king.

We adopt the officers. Tim is flight-property, the general boast: but John belongs to the three who valet his kite, Crasher to those other three, while Ginger is the object of my gang's service. We match our poppets and swap their virtues and vices in the hut of nights, as the airmen out east match their fighting scorpions and tarantulae.

8

WORK

Just as the roomy, sordid, clanging, momentous hangar is our cathedral, so our day's work in it is worship: and the one's as hard to rationalise as the other. There's a defiance of common-sense in every faith. We believe the job's worth every last lift of our arms and kick of our legs: and our belief, to outsiders, may well seem senseless as a Mass.

It's no slug's life we lead. Inside the hangar they keep us for the eight hours of an ordinary workshop: and before and after that there's our own cleaning, bed-making, hut-tidying: another hour and a half. Add, much grudged, an occasional hour wasted over equipment or bayonet for some posh parade: our monthly week on duty flight, when we stand by all the hundred and sixty-eight hours for emergency aerodrome occasions: fire-picket at night: a rare police guard, when we relieve the service police of some special responsibility: and you get a full life of work. Wednesday afternoons, Saturday afternoons and the few Sundays not desecrated by a parade service are golden spots in our laboriousness.

So much work, even when the work is worship, dulls the devotees. I get out of bed, often, as tired as I was at Depot: but so gratefully tired. And it passes off, for we all muck in:—the keenness of whoever feels fresh that morning whips up the

217

reluctant. When they fag us out, in Cadet College, it is at least upon the pith of life and not upon a surface adornment. We are greatly useful here in the eyes of all who accept our premiss, that the conquest of the air is the first duty of our generation.

The darling partiality of Nature, which has reserved across the ages her last element for us to dompt! By our handling of this, the one big new thing, will our time be judged. Incidentally, for the near-sighted or political, it has a national side: upon the start we give our successors in the arts of air will depend their redressing our eighteenth-century army and silly ships.

Don't imagine that we all feel this, or that this is all we feel. We face something whose scale towers out of our imaginations. Each of us knows that a hundred thousand men like him will work their hardest at it, for many lifetimes, and still not see an end. My loose loquacious mind gets so far in words. The extreme carefulness of our work gets further. It's not mercenary work, nor duty work. The Air Force and the pay are only fleas making our inspirations itch.

And don't fly away on the notion that I'd pretend us wonderful. We are everyday sinners, keyed to extreme action only because we're up against something bigger than ourselves: but we translate this into talk of nuts and bolts for the day's need. If one of our kites can't go up, for an avoidable reason, the flight hangs its head in disgrace. Suggest to Tug, there, that he's left something undone in his rigging: or tell Cap'n that his engine's not as well maintained as he can maintain it:—and then run for your life, if they think you serious.

When I passed from Depot to Cadet College I passed from appearance to reality. After two days I was saying I had found a home. At Depot we had soldiered so long and so harshly that soldiering had become second nature: sterility quickly beds

218

down into habit, by use. Now at Cadet College I was to learn to be an airman, by unlearning that corporate effort which had been the sole spirituality of the square.

It was a stress, the being chucked a job, and just bluntly told to get on with it. Taffy Jenkins had given us the detail of every movement, by numbers, for a joint performance at the word of command. Here they take intelligence for granted and are impatient with those who ask to learn. If we don't do the thing our way, sincerely, quickly and well enough, we're thrown out to something else. There's a ruthlessness with their human material that braces us: and a refreshingly high standard among the survivors. Our machines fly when they're as good as it lies in our power to make them. If that is not good enough, we drift to mess-deck fatigues or to sanitary squad: forfeiting the technical esteem of our pals. That is a harsh penalty, which puts poor Stiffy's extra drills far in the shade. There is no judgment so beyond appeal as the judgment of peers: and B Flight's a republic:—or would be, but for its willing obedience to King Tim.

9

FUNERAL

It was an odd morning, that on which we heard Queen Alexandra was dead. The fog which collects here on most autumn mornings was so shallow. Across the ground it lay like a veil: but when we looked up we could see a sparkle, which hinted at a sun almost shining upon the eaves and mast-heads. When we parade in fog, our figures go flat. There is no thickness, no shadows, no high-light of polished buttons. Instead the fellows are as if cut out of grey cardboard, with a darker tint drawn round the edges, where the shafts of refracted light slip round them.

We stood so, in our hollow square, this morning, while they hoisted colour, and played the daily salute for the King: but after the salute they held us at attention, ever so long in that dead shivering silence: for the air was very sharp. Then the ensign began to creep downward from the peak, while the massed drums of the band rolled. And they rolled and rolled all the minutes that the flag crept down. At half-mast the trumpets came out brazenly with the last post. We all swallowed our spittle, chokingly, while our eyes smarted against our wills. A man hates to be moved to folly by a noise.

They would not let us off the worst of it. There had to be a parade service the day she was buried. Our distrusted chaplain preached one of his questionable sermons. He spoke of the dead Queen as a Saint, a Paragon: not as an unfortunate, a long-suffering doll. With luscious mouth he enlarged upon her beauty, the beauty which God, in a marvel of loving-kindness, had let her keep until her dying.

My thoughts fled back sharply to Marlborough House. The yellow, scaling portal: the white-haired footmen and door-keepers, whiter than the powder of their hair: the hushed great barn-like halls: the deep carpet in which our feet dragged unwillingly to the ceiling-high fireplace which dwarfed the whispering Miss Knollys and Sir Dighton. She incredibly old, wasted, sallow: he a once huge man, whose palsied neck had let down the great head on the breast, where its gaping mouth wagged almost unseen and unheard in the thicket of beard which overgrew the waistcoat. Sir Dighton had won the first V.C. in the Crimea: and he was so old, and Miss Knollys so old that this seemed a cruel duty which kept them always on their feet. We whispered with them: everybody whispered in that charnel-house.

We had to wait, of course: that is the prerogative of Queens. When we reached the presence, and I saw the mummied thing, the bird-like head cocked on one side, not artfully but by disease, the red-rimmed eyes, the enamelled face, which the famous smile scissored across all angular and heart-rending:— then I nearly ran away in pity. The body should not be kept alive after the lamp of sense has gone out. There were the ghosts of all her lovely airs, the little graces, the once-effective sway and movement of the figure which had been her consolation. Her bony fingers, clashing in the tunnel of their rings, fiddled with albums, penholders, photographs, toys upon the table: and the heart-rending appeal played on us like a hose, more and more terribly. She soon dismissed us.

221

These memories lost me much of the sermon. I listened in again to hear the chaplain telling the story of Prince Albert Edward in the House of Lords warning Lord Granville he must miss part of his speech, because he had promised to take his daughter to the circus. 'This,' declaimed the padre, 'this was the domestic picture and example which the Prince and Princess of Wales set their adoring people.' 'Balls!' hissed someone, savagely, from behind me. In its thirty-second minute the sermon ended. More rolling of drums and last posts, now firmly resisted by all of us in our rage: and then back to dinner. 'Fall in at two for work!' shouted the Orderly Sergeant. 'Not even a half-holiday for the old girl,' grumbled Tug.

10

DANCE NIGHT

Chick came in first, just after eleven: but the strangeness of the empty hut made it feel like no time at all. The floor flickered and vanished, white and dark, like a waving flag, as my logs blazed up momently, or guttered away in smoke. He came in quickly, but the rubbers on his walking-out boots hushed his step, and he was careful not to wake me. For a moment he hesitated by his bed: flung down cap and stick, unhooked the choking collar of his tunic: then again he hesitated.

The fire rose, and caught his notice. He walked over, and seemed to extinguish it for a while, behind the black screen of his solidity. After, he began with lithe springing strides to pad up and down the wood-blocked floor, not noisily, but as though he loved the striding. He swung his arms, and once or twice muttered something, half-aloud, as he turned on his toes.

I rolled over in my bed, to warn him of my notice: he walked across, nuzzled down on my blankets, and bending his face (a strange scent) down to mine whispered, 'You awake, Ross?' I whispered back in my normal voice, reassuring him. He began to talk about the intoxication of the moon-lit frosty night, which filled his legs with dancing-love, like gin.

Suddenly he bent down again, muttering very gently, 'Do you know what happened to me, tonight? I met a girl . . . or she

223

wasn't a girl, really . . . and we . . . clicked and went off together. Remember that dollar I borrowed off you, Monday? Well that just did it.' He threw his hard weight flat along the narrow bed, whispering eagerly, 'You know blanket-drill, and what that feels like? Well, it's chalk to cheese. Made me jump, this did, like two hundred volts. I wondered if we'd go up in flames, like poor old Mouldy and his kite. I've come back in one run, without a breather. It's all of five miles, isn't it? Breeches and puttees: Christ, some run. Just you feel here and here: I'm sweating like a bull. You could wring my togs out. Don't think I can bug down tonight. Where's Tug? I can't ever do it the first time again: but Christ, it was bloody wonnerful.

'I say, what've I got to do now? Wash it, I s'pose. Got any dope?'

11

ON PARADE

The A.O.C., a very exalted person, strolled round our hollow square, half-hiding a yawn in his gloves, and scarcely letting the fact of us strike his withdrawn eye. Dolly (so we irreverently call him) has played his part in affairs: governed cities, planned battles, and conferred death on many hundreds of men. He enjoys the clash of idea, and such explorations of mind as go far and strangely. The set of another man's tunic seems to him mainly that man's affair. We like him, therefore, for our commanding officer: he is a type to picture; and to yarn of: also his aloof shyness allies itself to his memory of when things were real, to save us from over-much formality.

This inspection lasted only fifteen minutes. The wind blustered down our ranks, also inspecting us, but roughly. It brushed back the flap of the opposite flank's tunics (and of ours, no doubt, in their view), showing the lividly blue pocket-linings, underneath, and the top of each man's trousers. The sunlight caught the lifting or falling cloth at an angle, brightening it. So the still figures seemed to be all signalling together. This movement singularly destroyed the illusion we were set to give, of blue cylinders standing most stiffly, hardly breathing, eyes level and straight ahead.

The wind, taking no heed of our strain, blustered on, whipping sudden curves into the trouser-legs—long bows of curves, from groin to ankle, much deforming the semblance of legs inside. Meanwhile the Adjutant bear-led poor enduring Dolly down the three interminable lanes of us dressed ham-bones all tightly sewn up in bags of unvarying serge. Dolly was too civil to disappoint the Adjutant by saying No: and too decent-minded to scrutinise the reluctant flesh of his men, so paraded for judgment. Very soon came his famous final order. 'Cawwy on, Sergeant Major,' lisped with relief and a shy salute in our direction. Good old Dolly.

What a revenge that unwholesome depot takes on its victims! Any drill-order, even on these jocose parades, brings me back the hot odour of our panting flight, and the sound of Stiffy ramping up and down. An instinctive twitch of every nerve follows: and I square myself to hate drill with the hatred in which we hold the Depot. Stiffy's trying to hustle the young west has made the nascent R.A.F. unmilitary by deepest conviction. His square was an alien prelude. An airman at Depot was an airman being warped from nature. That unwholesome subjectitude, which he miscalled discipline, contained not even a root of the motives of service which enrich this place.

The Powers seem afraid to exploit this gravity, this devotion of a deadly purposefulness, which underlies our profession. Worse, they make themselves ridiculous by piping to us on the minor key of their panache. When five hundred airmen on parade see their officer march up to the Squadron Leader: (the two live together, as Ching and Alec, in the mess): see him halt with a click at the regulation distance, draw swellingly up, and salute like a pistol-shot—then five hundred airmen titter gently. It is theatrical, and theatre in England spells circus, and circus spells clown.

226 Perhaps, in days of Chivalry, even the north took the parade

of arms lovingly, ard throbbed at the feel of swords, the sight of banners. Perhaps: though I've chased through mediaeval literature after the days of chivalry, and found their revivals, and legends or reminiscences or ridicule of them, but never the real thing. Today these modes are right out of tune with the social system, whose firm-seatedness makes one doubt if an Englishman's blood can ever have flowed hotly enough for him to swallow a tomfoolery divorced from alcohol.

12

POLICE DUTY

Tonight, Saturday night, saw the end of summer time. So our tricks of sentry-go were an hour longer then military wont. It was strange to walk up and down, killing time, while time, or rather the clock, stood still. This camp is electric-clocked. At first the night was good, for the air (not too cold) was calm. All the camp slept, and there was no traffic on the roads. The transport-yard, our care, opens off the smoothly-tarred main road and is spacious. The moonlight filled it. Across the sky crept a thin haze, so transparent in the beginning that its translucency increased the brilliancy of the moon.

Gradually, as the mist thickened, the moon seemed to wane. Its rays struck upon the cliff of trees which bordered the far side of the road, rendering it more cliff-like, by flattening the planes of its height. The mist was yet dry, so that the light became dusty, and the trees were powdered grey with it. Grey trees, tied about their roots with a grey ribbon-wall of dry oölite slabs, well-fitted: and, shining through the copse (it not being thick enough to leaf over every chink) glowed the watch lamps of the power station, like beasts' eyes: while the transformer, which alone works at night, whined low or loud as it spun round.

The leaves, Autumn's first converts, were falling singly,

rarely, sadly, as though the trees were conscious of each loss. The moon and myself counted their fall. By the yard-gate the ragged leaves of a plane-tree lay upturned, so ashy-pale on the black grass edging of the road that they gathered the moon-light: and at first I thought them torn pages from a note-book.

The moon looked on, while I fitted words to what we saw. My vacant eyesight normally sees little: so when anything does get through the mind's preoccupation, at once I try to fix its form in phrases. Tonight I was fortunate, for one end of my beat turned by the alarm-lamp of the fire-station. I used its glow-light to note down the word or group of words which my mind and boots had hammered out on the patrol.

Later the night grew very cold. The chill of the earth soaked into me through the leather under my feet. The mist rallied and altogether hid the moon. My clothes became grey-haired with its wetness: also a longing for sleep weighed upon me, almost uncontrollably. When the clock at last moved again, and the hands crept forward to the half-hour of my relief, I was more than glad.

The hot air and light of the guard-room poisoned my face: even as the forced company of the service police, those vermin in the body of the R.A.F., poisoned my self-respect. They pushed free a seat for me on the form nearest the fire, and Shorty passed me his mug of cocoa, to thaw out my tongue. I had interrupted Corporal Payne, a sexual-smelling policeman, in the midst of retelling some adventures in London on last leave. So word-perfect was he (we do not ordinarily excel in fluency) that I suspected many previous tellings lay behind this tale.

The confusion of cold moonlight still weighed on me, and lost me much of his detail. I think his tart's bedroom must have been somewhere off Golden Square. She slept him on a couch, and would not let him into her bed, behind curtains in an al-cove: so while she was washing he peeped between: to see a dead infant lying on the counterpane. 'It was three days ago he died,' sobbed the girl.

The Corporal urged upon her the need to lose the body promptly. They wrapped it in brown paper, and took it to a neighbouring court, whose precipitous tenement-walls pushed London's night-cap of smoke and mist almost sky-far away, so that its arc refulgence hardly modified the blackness of the pit.

In the court's centre was a large drain, trap-covered, to shoot surface water away to the sewers. Payne felt round the grating, discovered the hinges, and pulled it open. He began to stuff in the body: but there seemed some obstacle. He kneeled to thrust his arm right down, and clear it: when a hand fell on his neck, and a loud voice said, 'Now what do you think you're doing in here?' It was the Orderly Sergeant, and he was asleep in his own bed in the police hut. 'My God, what a relief.'

13

THE WAY OF A BIRD

Airmen are so healthy and free of the joints, that they exult to fling their meat about. Activity does not remind them, yet, how man hangs in his body, crucified. So we drill hard, desperately hard, exercising our bodies. It is a kind of fun, just to pant them out. The raggedness of the mass-effort testifies that, after his own time, each man is caring to the utmost for his good health and muscularity.

Stiffy would have called it a rebellious caring, which tried more for movement than for combination, pretended towards individual benefit, and made his rhythms only a means to fitness. That centipede-lesson of a comity had been the occasional gold upon the slavery of depot. Slavery? We now called it soldiering, a strumpet-exhibitionism. The airman at Cadet College who dared try for excellence at drill was a bull-shitter, a bobber, a creeping cunt.

Stiffy has been superseded by the new redeeming standard of a job to live by. In its virtue we resist the gas of militarism, which is breathed at us by our sergeants:—eight in ten of whom are old soldiers or old sailors, transferred in authority to the R.A.F. till the baby service has bred its own veterans. They do their best with us men-in-the-moon, do these old minds, which were set before ever they transferred: but we and they speak different languages: their traditional eyes cannot even see how far from their pasts we have diverged.

Airmen estimate in terms of their trades. The overwhelming responsibility our generation lays on us is that our kites and engines must always be airworthy, to take our masters and ourselves into the air. If these masters so interpret their duty as to break into work-hours with drill, then are they so much less our masters: but we must not complain except privily. It is for the public, which pays them and us, to see to it. Besides perhaps they are like cunning old Tim who vexes us with bull-shit if he sees a trace of dirt on the machines. After a minute on the square how excellent is work, how real!

A touch of punishment for slackness in duty:—yes, that's drill's reasonable function. Men will never work for long, unpunished: but punishment, for the thin-skinned, must be feather-light, only perceptible by the victim in its after-effects. But if the Powers blunder and ask that a drill be done well, for its own sake: or for a decoration, to smarten our bearing:— why then the body politic festers. We instinctively work canny, resisting within bounds to checkmate the enemy. At least so we intend: but all of us aren't saints enough or clever enough to stop in the right place. Our light-weights will go wicked and take their revenge out of the innocent work, identifying their splendid service with some trumpery drill-maniac.

The hard names show how we are moved. At Cadet College was an abortion (we called it the clockwork lobster) for whom the poetry and high feeling and zest in achievement of the irks were so many devils to be hammered out of them by discipline. When Dolly gave his lobster a yard of line, these complainants of ours would go slow in the workshop not merely on the day of drill (we all did that, in nausea. It is bitter to be betrayed by an officer of our own service) but on the day before and on

232

the day after, too. Happily the greater part saw it was bad form so to betray that the atom could anger us.

Against these few bolshies, the fellows of my kidney would struggle fiercely, preaching submission: even, if necessary, as low as the Depot point of sterilising ourselves to await orders for everything. Let the militarists have their way to its nth of futility. Time played into our hands. If the technical men held together and, ruefully smiling, offered both cheeks and the conduct of their handicrafts to discipline, why in no time the whole freedom of the future would be forced on them, by the discovery that the soldier and the mechanic were mutually destructive ideals. As the art of flying grew richer, the trade must deepen in mystery, or go under—and there could be no failure for the R.A.F. with the material now accepting enlistment. It had grown bigger than its rank and file, bigger than its chiefs.

The officers might delay progress for a few years: no more. Even now the airmen called the tune, in work-hours. A spanner, a screwdriver, a scraper, a file—these are our insignia: not the plumed wings, the swords, the eagles. There compete for our respect the officers who order the public carriage of our canes, and those who design new aircraft, or authorise two extra thou of backlash in the planet pinions of an epi-gear. Which will win the suffrage of fellows as trade-proud as ourselves? Yet the first sort think to bully it with high chins over us on parade, while the others are round-shouldered, shy, and scruffy with oil-stains. A parting of the roads!

It is a real danger. In this new service there can be nothing more traditional than the immemorial crafts: nothing so human as the mechanic off duty: nothing sentimental except a rare pantomime at Wembley or Hendon. The working mechanic will not be gay, with the weight of the effort towards indefinite victory on his unguided head:—unguided, largely because the

Officers' Mess achieves the public-school tone, and so dares not look beyond the concrete.

Those we regard as our natural aristocracy show three generations of artisan forbears by their mere grip of the tool-handle. Lacking this touch, though you're the best fellow in the world, you cannot be our leader. A pilot climbs into one of our busses, yanks the throttle open and flogs her into the air. Hear us curse his ham-fisted cruelty to machines. Our machines, please: the beloved created things whose every inmost bolt or outstretched spar has felt our caring fingers. Many officers know only the back and bottom cushions of their cockpit seats. 'Officers? I've shit 'em,' rigger or fitter will choke out over there, angered nearly to tears.

14

CLASSES

The Air Ministry recognises a rightness in our worship of the technical engineer, by promoting sergeant or sergeant-pilot the best men from the ranks: those who have understanding of the souls of engines, and find their poetry in the smooth tick-over.

They form our aristocracy of merit. Against them, over them, stand the lords spiritual, the commissioned: whose dignity comes extrinsically, from some fancied laying-on of hands. When they are forceful souls, Tims or Taffys, one to a squad, all is well. The basic lesion of character in every enlisted man makes him ready to laugh or cry, always, like a child: but seldom leaves him sober. So the hand of a father seems neither incongruous nor disagreeable to us. We earn force, by our root-folly.

Our conscious inferiority excludes Tim from comparison or challenge: but there is rising up a second category of airman, the boy apprentice. They disrupt us now: for the men don't like the boys: but this inevitable phase is a passing phase. Soon the ex-boy will be the majority, and the R.A.F. I knew will be superseded and forgotten. Meanwhile there is jealousy and carping.

The boys come fresh from school, glib in theory, essay

writers, with the bench-tricks of workmen: but they have never done the real job on a real kite: and reality, carrying responsibility, has a different look and feel from a school lesson. So they are put for a year to work with men. An old rigger, with years of service, whose trade is in his fingers, finds himself in charge of a boy-beginner with twice his pay. The kid is clever with words, and has passed out L.A.C. from school: the old hand can hardly spell, and will be for ever an A.C.2. He teaches his better ever so grumpily.

Nor do all the ex-boys make the job easier for those they are about to replace. As a class they are cocky. Remember how we, the enlisted men, have all been cowed. Behind us, in our trial of civvy life, is the shadow of failure. Bitterly we know, of experience, that we are not as good as the men outside. So officers, sergeants and corporals may browbeat us, and we'll lie down to it: even fawn on them the more for it. That sense of inferiority may not save us from the smart of discipline (your bully will always find his way to be severe, if it's merely to put the fear of God in us) but it gives us the humility of house-dogs, under discipline.

The airmen of the future will not be so owned, body and soul, by their service. Rather will they be the service, maintaining it, and their rights in it, as one with the officers. Whereas we have had no rights, except on paper, and few there. In the old days men had weekly to strip off boots and socks, and expose their feet for an officer's inspection. An ex-boy'd kick you in the mouth, as you bent down to look. So with the bath-rolls, a certificate from your N.C.O. that you'd had a bath during the week. One bath! And with the kit inspections, and room inspections, and equipment inspections, all excuses for the dogmatists among the officers to blunder, and for the nosy-parkers

236

to make beasts of themselves. Oh, you require the gentlest touch to interfere with a poor man's person, and not give offence.

The ex-boys are professionally in the R.A.F. as a privilege, making it their home. Soon, when they have made their style felt, officers will only enter their airmen's rooms accompanied, by invitation, guest-like and bare-headed, like us in an officers' mess. Officers will not be allowed to slough their uniform for social functions, while airmen walk about branded everywhere. The era of a real partnership in our very difficult achievement must come, if progress is to be lasting.

15

FUGITIVE

My Cadet College notes shortened, grew occasional, stopped. Months and months flowed silently away. I think I had become happy. 'Why,' complained E.M.F., 'as the years pass, do I find that word harder and harder to write?' Because when we write we are not happy: we only recollect it: and a recollection of the exceeding subtlety of happiness has something of the infect, unlawful: it being an overdraft on life.

If happiness was vested in ourselves, we could make it our habit, by selfishly shutting ourselves away: though this complete peacefulness of the restricted circle is not to compare with the half-peace of a wider one: but happiness, while primarily dependent on our internal balance of desire and opportunity, lies also at the mercy of our external acquaintance. One jar in all the circumambient—and our day is out of tune.

We, in the service, if a good time comes, snatch at it: knowing that blind chance has overlooked us sports of circumstance for the moment. Cadet College, during my spell, was passing through such a golden weather: and B Flight was probably the best of Cadet College. Look up from the bottom as high as we could, even to the A.O.C., and each degree of our commanders was benignant. We were fortunate in Tim, fortunate in our sergeant and corporal. Within the hut we were free and equal. Troops can exist in harmony by tolerating one another. In B Flight we were luckier than that. We liked one another.

There was a quality of desperation about this liking. We knew our transience. The flight was as fugitive and feeble as a summer cloud. Every week some rumour of change would shake our trust. Every month or so a change would take effect. For the days before it we would go about—knowing that old Tug was posted, trying to estimate what we should specially miss in old Tug: and the new man? Who would he be? How would he muck-in?

I shall not forget the black despair which overwhelmed me as the day approached of my own going into self-appointed exile, to save my R.A.F. skin from the repercussion of a folly in 1918. I lost, then, the best home and companionship of my forty years' living. I wonder who took my place? In a society of twelve, each player has a solo importance, and a bad man will spoil the whole. For three weeks we had an unfitting sergeant, who turned the best-pleased and best-working flight of Cadet College to rebellious misery. The fortune of an airman is gossamer, disordered by a single breath, and his life poignant, from its fragility.

Of course we strive to mitigate the evil. A first instinct of existence teaches us to sacrifice everything which might endanger our solidity. Twelve men in a constricted bedroom:— indeed we cannot afford the luxury of our own angles. The ideal of troops is to be as like and close-fitting as bee cells. If one dislikes another, and shows it, the flight will be out of joint: and the egg-shell of its comfort crack. We so cultivate the face of friendliness that from a mask it becomes a habit, from a habit conviction. To preserve it we jettison our realities . . . or cover them so deep that we fail to hear their voice. In the hut no point is put without qualification, no opinion

239

pressed far enough to hurt. We run on half-throttle, in company.

This constriction within doors demands a venturesome outlet elsewhere. Out of it comes a degree of the heat and heart of our work. Out of it, too, comes our passion for games. In the practical argument of football a fellow can do his damnedest, giving and taking knocks; can be gloriously reckless of mud, and of his clothes and his body. To live as hard as we play would make life earnest. Those who do not play can find an escape in immoderate social exercise among the neighbouring towns and villages. A few find it in the wet bar of the canteen.

16

THE ROAD

The extravagance in which my surplus emotion expressed itself lay on the road. So long as roads were tarred blue and straight; not hedged; and empty and dry, so long I was rich.

Nightly I'd run up from the hangar, upon the last stroke of work, spurring my tired feet to be nimble. The very movement refreshed them, after the day-long restraint of service. In five minutes my bed would be down, ready for the night: in four more I was in breeches and puttees, pulling on my gauntlets as I walked over to my bike, which lived in a garage-hut, opposite. Its tyres never wanted air, its engine had a habit of starting at second kick: a good habit, for only by frantic plunges upon the starting pedal could my puny weight force the engine over the seven atmospheres of its compression.

Boanerges' first glad roar at being alive again nightly jarred the huts of Cadet College into life. 'There he goes, the noisy bugger,' someone would say enviously in every flight. It is part of an airman's profession to be knowing with engines: and a thoroughbred engine is our undying satisfaction. The camp wore the virtue of my Brough like a flower in its cap. Tonight Tug and Dusty came to the step of our hut to see me off. 'Running down to Smoke, perhaps?' jeered Dusty; hitting at my regular game of London and back for tea on fine Wednesday afternoons.

Boa is a top-gear machine, as sweet in that as most single-cylinders in middle. I chug lordly past the guard-room and through the speed limit at no more than sixteen. Round the bend, past the farm, and the way straightens. Now for it. The engine's final development is fifty-two horse-power. A miracle that all this docile strength waits behind one tiny lever for the pleasure of my hand.

Another bend: and I have the honour of one of England's straightest and fastest roads. The burble of my exhaust unwound like a long cord behind me. Soon my speed snapped it, and I heard only the cry of the wind which my battering head split and fended aside. The cry rose with my speed to a shriek: while the air's coldness streamed like two jets of iced water into my dissolving eyes. I screwed them to slits, and focused my sight two hundred yards ahead of me on the empty mosaic of the tar's gravelled undulations.

Like arrows the tiny flies pricked my cheeks: and sometimes a heavier body, some house-fly or beetle, would crash into face or lips like a spent bullet. A glance at the speedometer: seventy-eight. Boanerges is warming up. I pull the throttle right open, on the top of the slope, and we swoop flying across the dip, and up-down up-down the switchback beyond: the weighty machine launching itself like a projectile with a whirr of wheels into the air at the take-off of each rise, to land lurchingly with such a snatch of the driving chain as jerks my spine like a rictus.

Once we so fled across the evening light, with the yellow sun on my left, when a huge shadow roared just overhead. A Bristol Fighter, from Whitewash Villas, our neighbour aerodrome, was banking sharply round. I checked speed an instant

to wave: and the slip-stream of my impetus snapped my arm
and elbow astern, like a raised flail. The pilot pointed down
the road towards Lincoln. I sat hard in the saddle, folded back
my ears and went away after him, like a dog after a hare.
Quickly we drew abreast, as the impulse of his dive to my level
exhausted itself.

The next mile of road was rough. I braced my feet into the
rests, thrust with my arms, and clenched my knees on the tank
till its rubber grips goggled under my thighs. Over the first pot-
hole Boanerges screamed in surprise, its mud-guard bottoming
with a yawp upon the tyre. Through the plunges of the next
ten seconds I clung on, wedging my gloved hand in the throttle
lever so that no bump should close it and spoil our speed. Then
the bicycle wrenched sideways into three long ruts: it swayed
dizzily, wagging its tail for thirty awful yards. Out came the
clutch, the engine raced freely: Boa checked and straightened
his head with a shake, as a Brough should.

The bad ground was passed and on the new road our flight
became birdlike. My head was blown out with air so that my
ears had failed and we seemed to whirl soundlessly between
the sun-gilt stubble fields. I dared, on a rise, to slow impercep-
tibly and glance sideways into the sky. There the Bif was, two
hundred yards and more back. Play with the fellow? Why not?
I slowed to ninety: signalled with my hand for him to overtake.
Slowed ten more: sat up. Over he rattled. His passenger, a
helmeted and goggled grin, hung out of the cock-pit to pass
me the 'Up yer' Raf randy greeting.

They were hoping I was a flash in the pan, giving them
best. Open went my throttle again. Boa crept level, fifty feet
below: held them: sailed ahead into the clean and lonely country. An approaching car pulled nearly into its ditch at the sight
of our race. The Bif was zooming among the trees and tele-

graph poles, with my scurrying spot only eighty yards ahead. I gained though, gained steadily: was perhaps five miles an hour the faster. Down went my left hand to give the engine two extra dollops of oil, for fear that something was running hot: but an overhead Jap twin, super-tuned like this one, would carry on to the moon and back, unfaltering.

We drew near the settlement. A long mile before the first houses I closed down and coasted to the cross-roads by the hospital. Bif caught up, banked, climbed and turned for home, waving to me as long as he was in sight. Fourteen miles from camp, we are, here: and fifteen minutes since I left Tug and Dusty at the hut door.

I let in the clutch again, and eased Boanerges down the hill, along the tram-lines through the dirty streets and up-hill to the aloof cathedral, where it stood in frigid perfection above the cowering close. No message of mercy in Lincoln. Our God is a jealous God: and man's very best offering will fall disdainfully short of worthiness, in the sight of Saint Hugh and his angels.

Remigius, earthy old Remigius, looks with more charity on me and Boanerges. I stabled the steel magnificence of strength and speed at his west door and went in: to find the organist practising something slow and rhythmical, like a multiplication table in notes, on the organ. The fretted, unsatisfying and unsatisfied lace-work of choir screen and spandrels drank in the main sound. Its surplus spilled thoughtfully into my ears.

By then my belly had forgotten its lunch, my eyes smarted and streamed. Out again, to sluice my head under the White Hart's yard-pump. A cup of real chocolate and a muffin at the teashop: and Boa and I took the Newark road for the last hour of daylight. He ambles at forty-five and when roaring his utmost, surpasses the hundred. A skittish motor-bike with a touch of blood in it is better than all the riding animals on earth, because of its logical extension of our faculties, and the hint, the provocation, to excess conferred by its honeyed untiring smoothness. Because Boa loves me, he gives me five more miles of speed than a stranger would get from him.

At Nottingham I added sausages from my wholesaler to the bacon which I'd bought at Lincoln: bacon so nicely sliced that each rasher meant a penny. The solid pannier-bags behind the saddle took all this and at my next stop (a farm) took also a felt-hammocked box of fifteen eggs. Home by Sleaford, our squalid, purse-proud, local village. Its butcher had six penn'orth of dripping ready for me. For months have I been making my evening round a marketing, twice a week, riding a hundred miles for the joy of it and picking up the best food cheapest, over half the country side.

17

A THURSDAY NIGHT

The fire is a cooking fire, red between the stove-bars, all its flame and smoke burned off. Half-past eight. The other ten fellows are yarning in a blue haze of tobacco, two on the chairs, eight on the forms, waiting my return. After the clean night air their cigarette smoke gave me a coughing fit. Also the speed of my last whirling miles by lamplight (the severest test of riding) had unsteadied my legs, so that I staggered a little. "Wo-ups, dearie,' chortled Dusty. 'More split-arse work to-night?' It pleases them to imagine me wild on the road. To feed this flight-vanity I gladden them with details of my scrap against the Bif.

'Bring any grub?' at length enquires Nigger, whose pocket is too low, always, for canteen. I knew there was something lacking. The excitement of the final dash and my oncoming weariness had chased from my memory the stuffed panniers of the Brough. Out into the night again, steering across the black garage to the corner in which he is stabled by the fume of hot iron rising from his sturdy cylinders. Click, click, the bags are detached; and I pour out their contents before Dusty, the hut pantry-man. Tug brings out the frying pan, and has precedency. The first is just right for it. A sizzle and a filling smell. I get ready my usual two slices of buttered toast.

Nigger turns over the possibilities. 'What are eggs?' he asks. I do a lightning calculation: penny ha'penny. Right: he chooses one egg. Rashers are a penny. Two of them and two dogs, at tuppence. He rolls me his sixpence along the table. 'Keep the odd 'un for fat,' he murmurs. The others choose and pay. Selling the stuff is no trouble: we have run this supper scandal among ourselves all the winter. The canteen food is dearer, though not dear; and much less tasteful than these fruits of our own fetching and cooking. And you have to queue up there, for ten minutes, to be pertly served.

Paddy, the last cooker of tonight, cleans the pan for tomorrow by wiping out its dripping on a huge doorstep of mess-deck bread. Later we'll see him put this bread to belly-use. 'Old grease-trap,' Tug calls him, rallyingly. Meanwhile the gramophone plays jazz stuff to charm down the food. My brain is too dishevelled after a hard ride to be fit for string-music, its dope of a wet evening. For tonight I am drowsy-drunk on air. Lights out finds us all willing for sleep. Tomorrow the golden eagle moults on us.

18

INTERLUDE

Service life in this way teaches a man to live largely on little. We belong to a big thing, which will exist for ever and ever in unnumbered generations of standard airmen, like ourselves. Our outward samenesses of dress and type remind us of that. Also our segregation and concentration. The clusters of us widen out beyond Cadet College, beyond Whitewash Villas, beyond Depot, over hundreds of camps, over half the world. The habit of 'belonging to something or other' induces in us a sense of being one part of many things.

As we gain attachment, so we strip ourselves of personality. Mark the spiritual importance of such trifles as these overalls in which we shroud ourselves for work, like robots: to become drab shapes without comeliness or particularity, and careless, careless. The clothes for which a fellow has to pay are fetters to him, unless he is very rich and spendthrifty. This working dress provided us by the R.A.F. is not the least of our freedoms. When we put it on, oil, water, mud, paint, all such hazardous things, are instantly our friends.

A spell of warm weather has come back to us, as if summer feared to quit this bleak north. The wind keeps its bite; but our hangar shelters a calm crescent of tarmac and grass, and its open mouth is a veritable sun-trap. Through the afternoon eight of us lay there waiting for a kite which had gone away south, across country, and was overdue. Wonderful, to have it for our duty to do nothing but wait hour after hour in the warm sunshine, looking out southward.

We were too utterly content to speak, drugged with an absorption fathoms deeper than physical contentment. Just we lay there spread-eagled in a mesh of bodies, pillowed on one another and sighing in happy excess of relaxation. The sunlight poured from the sky and melted into our tissues. From the turf below our moist backs there came up a sister-heat which joined us to it. Our bones dissolved to become a part of this underlying indulgent earth, whose mysterious pulse throbbed in every tremor of our bodies. The scents of the thousand-acre drome mixed with the familiar oil-breath of our hangar, nature with art: while the pale sea of the grass bobbed in little waves before the wind raising a green surf which hissed and flowed by the slats of our heat-lidded eyes.

Such moments of absorption resolve the mail and plate of our personality back into the carbo-hydrate elements of being. They come to service men very often, because of our light surrender to the good or evil of the moment.

Airmen have no possessions, few ties, little daily care. For me, duty now orders only the brightness of these five buttons down my front.

And airmen are cared for as little as they care. Their simple eyes, out-turned; their natural living; the penurious imaginations which neither harrow nor reap their lowlands of mind: all these expose them, like fallows, to the processes of air. In the summer we are easily the sun's. In winter we struggle undefended along the roadway, and the rain and wind chivy us, till soon we are wind and rain. We race over in the first dawn to the College's translucent swimming pool, and dive into the elastic water which fits our bodies closely as a skin:—and we belong to that too. Everywhere a relationship: no loneliness any more.

I can't write 'Finis' to this book, while I am still serving. I hope, sometimes, that I will never write it.

In the Norton Library

CRITICISM AND THE HISTORY OF IDEAS